The Art of Teaching Secondary English

What is the art of teaching secondary English?

At a time when school-based English is becoming reductive and mechanistic, the authors of this book reconsider the fundamental philosophy of English teaching, evaluate current practice and offer a practical framework for new approaches to teaching this important subject.

The authors draw on recent initiatives in the area, including the National Literacy Strategy, but offer also wider perspectives on the formation and development of both English and English teaching in a modern society. This will help teachers develop both a personal philosophy and a critical perspective on the various traditions of English teaching as well as on current initiatives and reforms. The book includes:

- provocative quotations from writers, artists and thinkers;
- responses from key figures in modern educational thought;
- exploration and development of the principle areas, illuminating key issues, tensions and opportunities;
- practical possibilities for classroom practice.

The Art of Teaching Secondary English is a practical and accessible resource for everyone involved in English teaching, including teachers and student teachers of English.

David Stevens is Senior Lecturer in Education at the University of Durham. **Nicholas McGuinn** is Lecturer in Educational Studies at the University of York.

The Art of Teaching Secondary English

Innovative and creative approaches

David Stevens and
Nicholas McGuinn

RoutledgeFalmer
Taylor & Francis Group

LONDON AND NEW YORK

BOWLING GREEN STATE
UNIVERSITY LIBRARIES

First published 2004
by RoutledgeFalmer
11 New Fetter Lane, London EC4P 4EE

Simultaneously published in the USA and Canada
by RoutledgeFalmer
29 West 35th Street, New York, NY 10001

RoutledgeFalmer is an imprint of the Taylor & Francis Group

© 2004 David Stevens and Nicholas McGuinn

Typeset in Sabon by
Florence Production Ltd, Stoodleigh, Devon
Printed and bound in Great Britain by
TJ International Ltd, Padstow, Cornwall

All rights reserved. No part of this book may be reprinted
or reproduced or utilised in any form or by any electronic,
mechanical, or other means, now known or hereafter invented,
including photocopying and recording, or in any information
storage or retrieval system, without permission in writing
from the publishers.

British Library Cataloguing in Publication Data
A catalogue record for this book is available from the British
Library

Library of Congress Cataloging in Publication Data
A catalog record for this book has been requested

ISBN 0–415–29858–X (hbk)
ISBN 0–415–29859–8 (pbk)

Contents

Acknowledgements

September Song, 14 lines (p. 67) from *Collected Poems* by Geoffrey Hill (first published in *King Log* 1968, Penguin Books, 1985). Copyright © Geoffrey Hill, 1968, 1985 (for UK and Commonwealth excluding Canada).

September Song, from *New & Collected Poems*, 1952–1992 by Geoffrey Hill. Copyright © 1994 by Geoffrey Hill. Reprinted by permission of Houghton Mifflin Company. All rights reserved. (For United States, its territories and dependencies, and the Open Market.)

Extract from *Autogeddon* by Heathcote Williams published by Jonathan Cape. Used by permission of The Random House Group Limited.

Extract from *Letter to Daniel* by Fergal Keane published by Penguin. Used by permission of David Sodwin Associates.

Extract from *Them & [Uz]* by Tony Harrison reprinted with permission of the author. Selected Poems, Penguin, 1995.

Sections of Chapters 1, 2 and 6 first appeared, in shorter versions, in Stevens, D. 'English for the English: an Intercultural Approach', in Alred, Byram and Fleming (eds) *Intercultural Experience and Education* (Clevedon: Multilingual Matters, 2003), and in Stevens, D. 'William Blake in Education' (in *Changing English* 7:1; 2000).

Don Salter read early drafts of several chapters, and made helpful, encouraging suggestions.

Introduction

We have aimed, here, to write a polemical but at the same time often practically oriented book intended for English teachers, lecturers in university departments of education and student teachers of English at all levels, developing and adapting a fundamentally Romantic notion of the subject English. In one sense this is a rediscovery, a restoration perhaps, of the root traditions of the subject as a counter to recurring reductive and mechanistic tendencies in school-based English. In another sense, though, we present what we hope is a robust response to the urgent challenges of the new millennium in the context of such areas as the intercultural connections and responsibilities of English teaching, ICT possibilities, extending literacies, and the place of the arts in the curriculum.

In a telling phrase, the writer David Almond has described the essence of good writing – and, by implication, of the subject English itself – as *practical magic*. In this book we examine both parts of the definition, recognising the inherent tensions between them, but also their complementary nature if English teaching is to develop imaginatively. Similarly, we look at notions of subjectivity – the traditions of individual responses to language or literary stimuli at the centre of English – and objectivity – the demonstrable need to improve standards of basic and critical literacy. Again, we shall seek to establish a new synthesis, based on reflection and speculation derived from our own and others' empirical research.

Each chapter is structured along broadly similar lines, to include substantial and provocative quotations from writers, artists and thinkers in the English Romantic tradition and responses from key figures in the modern context of educational thought and practice. There is substantial exploration and development of the principal areas raised, reflecting on and illuminating the key issues, tensions and opportunities, together with some indication of the arising practical possibilities based on research among teachers, student teachers and pupils of English. The focus here is on the implications of the presented ideas, as outlined, on the potential for subsequent classroom practice.

Throughout, we reflect on the possible meanings of the Romantic tradition through some of its chief exponents, and on its implications for practice. We look at some of the pedagogical variants of English as they have developed, especially in the light of interactive approaches to learning, the uses of exploratory play, and the status of English as a fundamentally arts-based discipline. Especially significant here is what might be termed the intercultural dimension of native language teaching – English, for our purposes – made urgently significant by the developing nature of English as possible *lingua franca* in a multi-cultural world both within the classroom and far beyond. We draw especially on Critical Pedagogy (CP) in its possible relationship to Romanticism, particularly with reference to Freire's helpful radical distinction between 'banking' and holistic concepts of education. The broad context for all this features the varied, often nebulous, power relationships in language and schooling: concepts of critical literacy, citizenship and justice in education as perceived in the structures and competing discourses of schooling.

In many ways, the core of effective English teaching may be seen as the centrally Romantic idea of wonder as the essence of art (and of poetry particularly, perhaps) – seeing the familiar in new ways – and, by extension, of all that is celebratory and enlightening in the best traditions of English teaching. In this context, however, we are also concerned to emphasise the critical as well as the celebratory possibilities, and we draw on such notions as Brechtian de-familiarisation, Bruner's idea of teaching as 'violating expectancy', and Wittgenstein's perception of the inherent strangeness of language itself. Important, too, is the developing – and often uncertain – impact of new technologies upon the ways in which texts are created, mediated and received: the liberating possibilities and inevitable constraints in their realisation. Ultimately, we examine compromises, opportunities and subversions – sometimes all together – in the context of the legislated curriculum and its policing.

This amounts to no elaborate ivory-tower exercise; between us we have spent our professional lives teaching English in eight different schools, four as Head of English, and now work closely with student teachers of English and with colleagues in partnership schools and university departments of education. We recognise the often harsh realities of the educational climate in which we live; the idea for this book, indeed, derives from this recognition.

We have tried, further, to model some of the aspects of English teaching that we commend in the way we have collaborated in the writing of this book. Each of us speaks with a particular voice – the authorship of each chapter is made explicit for this reason – but, at the same time, we have worked closely together to make what we hope are valid, productive connections. We have also assembled a large number of other voices, through quotations and references, to amplify and elucidate the central ideas. Sometimes, for English teachers, these voices are presented in rather unusual contexts or juxtapositions, and in this we hope that readers may encounter new thinkers, or more familiar ones seen in a new light. In all this, clearly, there is what is essentially an intercultural venture.

David Stevens, University of Durham
Nicholas McGuinn, University of York

1 The arts of English teaching

I give you the end of a golden string,
Only wind it into a ball,
It will lead you in at Heaven's gate
Built in Jerusalem's wall.
   William Blake, from 'Jerusalem'

Even more than usual, writing this book is no easy matter. Secondary-level English teaching in England and Wales at the start of the twenty-first century appears to be in a state of some confusion. In our experience, its practitioners often feel beset by internal philosophical and practical divisions, and by externally formulated governmental and quasi-governmental policies and targets. In the context of this book especially, offering an essentially Romantic conception of the nature of English teaching and learning, there arise particularly contentious – and fiercely contested – assertions, issues and tensions.

The vast majority of practising English teachers and student teachers continue to be drawn to creative, inspirational models of English teaching, as underlined by recent research (Marshall 2000; Marshall *et al.* 2001), and by countless professional conversations with practising and preparing English teachers. Yet, it is precisely these pedagogical models which are frequently perceived to be under threat in what may be seen as an overcrowded, over-prescribed, over-tested curriculum overly focused on basic literacy. As Ellis (2002: 1) puts it:

> The prodigious volume of initiatives, frameworks, standards, audits, skills tests, performance indicators and all the other monstrous paraphernalia of a technocratic, accountability-obsessed bureaucracy have truly destructive effects; they sap teachers' creative energies, they regard the teaching of reading and writing as a science (in which we can guarantee exactly what effect X or Y will have on children) and they disengage individual teachers from a community of shared knowledge and values ... that gives us a sense of purpose and an identity.

Whether this kind of perception is justified – and if so in what ways and how much – is part of the purpose of this book. Our larger intention is to formulate and demonstrate positive theoretical and practical responses to the current climate, building on diverse but complementary approaches to the arts of English teaching. In other words, to find ways of remaining creatively engaged with English teaching while working with – or on occasion subverting – the various initiatives handed down to us. We are essentially concerned with re-positioning English, and certainly not with replacing it: on the contrary, as we experience more and more complex issues of language and meaning across fast-multiplying textual genres, more than ever the subject should be seen as the centrepiece of the curriculum.

So much depends on our overall aims as English teachers: what exactly are our overarching intentions in the classroom and beyond? Beyond the establishment of basic, functional literacy (and even this notion is complicated and contentious), what kind of education are we offering to tomorrow's adult citizens? The particular social, linguistic, technological, intercultural complexities of life at the start of the twenty-first century make for a certain urgency in at least reflecting on tentative responses to these questions. The National Curriculum (DfEE 1999) itself, in its all too often ignored preamble presenting 'Values, Aims and Purposes', is interesting in this context. Following a statement of fundamental values, the document goes on to elaborate on two basic aims: the first, dealing with opportunities to learn and achieve, concludes that: 'the curriculum should enable pupils to think creatively and critically . . . to make a difference for the better. It should give them the opportunity to become creative, innovative, enterprising and capable of leadership'.

The second aim endorses spiritual, moral, social and cultural education, including the development of pupils' 'knowledge, understanding and appreciation of their own and different beliefs and cultures, and how these influence individuals and societies' (DfEE/QCA 1999: 11).

Statements such as these are rich with significance for English teaching and, legally and ethically, lie at the very heart of the curriculum. In terms of creativity, critical thinking and intercultural understanding they also provide important principles for the present book.

But issues like these are certainly not new. The English poet and prose writer Thomas Traherne (1637–1674), for example, described both the opportunities and limitations of his own highly privileged Oxford education. In one of the autobiographical sections of his seminal work, *Centuries*, Traherne discusses these contradictions; having initially paid tribute to the breadth of learning possible at this august university,

> Nevertheless some things were defective too. There was never a tutor that did professly teach Felicity, though that be the mistress of all other sciences. Nor did any of us study those things but as aliena, which we

ought to have studied as our enjoyments. We studied to inform our knowledge but knew not for what end we so studied. And for lack of aiming at a certain end we erred in the manner.

(Century 3, 37)

So, for Traherne, mere knowledge without a strong sense of purpose is clearly insufficient: it leaves people unrealised, unsatisfied, seventeenth-century Oxford students of divinity or twenty-first-century teachers and learners of English, perhaps, alike. The relevance is striking, if the terminology perhaps unfamiliar. Traherne's notion of 'felicity' is the full, active and celebratory enjoyment of life: his vision of the world is powerfully child-like and profoundly personal; and yet it espouses the potential of others too, precisely because of its subjectivity:

> You never enjoy the world aright, till the sea tself floweth in your veins, till you are clothed with the heavens and crowned with the stars: and perceive yourself to be the sole heir of the whole world, and more than so, because men are in it *who are every one sole heirs as well as you.*

(Century 1, 29, my italics)

That a sense of wonder at the nature of existence may be combined with a strongly critical and reflective standpoint, and that both these distanced positions may complement active, engaged immersion in teaching and learning, are key ideas of this book. In effect, this is what the notion of felicity means in the context of the twenty-first century. The implications of these combinations will be explored in a range of contexts, helping to illuminate the particular issues involved in the teaching of English as a native language. One tension being explored here is that between engaged involvement on the one hand, and critical, reflective distance on the other. As a traditional Sufi saying advises: 'be in the world, not of the world'. In a sense, of course, this tension is at the heart of any creative act, any artistic endeavour – and it is our contention that teaching – of English in this instance – is, essentially, an art. Ideally, the sense of involvement is the powerful motivating force in teaching and learning, and the sense of critical distance leads to greater understanding. Both are essential. And both derive their power, broadly, from a Romantic position. The purpose is critically to challenge prejudice – even when it is effectively prejudice couched in the everyday language of 'common sense', just as the scientific discipline of sociology, for example, seeks to deconstruct and question common-sense views about the nature of individuals and society. In this sense, the subject English is especially significant, beyond the generic concerns of teaching and learning which affect all disciplines, in its sharp focus on language – how it both expresses and conceals meaning, often simultaneously. For, as

Wittgenstein (in Kenny 1994: 24) reminded us, 'the limits of my language mean the limits of my world', but that word 'limits' is, itself, a slippery one, contentious and open to various interpretations. In an important sense – certainly important for the intentions of the English classroom – for 'limits' we could read 'infinite possibilities of meaning', for that is precisely how language operates.

Broad notions – of awe and wonder on the one hand, and of critical, evaluative distance on the other – were taken up a century or so after Traherne's time by many of the Romantics, although it is the former position that has come widely to characterise Romanticism. As Abbs has noted (1976: 5), the very roots of English as a subject are embedded in 'the tougher side of Romanticism' – the celebratory and the critical complementing each other – and it seems timely now to re-establish, and develop, this foundation. The important principle is in the discovery *and* in the making of meaning. In this context, subjectivity (the intensely personal) and objectivity (the social and cultural context which enables meanings to be explored and found) should be held to be mutually beneficial rather than mutually exclusive as is often, and damagingly, supposed. An important principle in the English classroom is that of 'informed subjectivity': an acknowledgement – a celebration, indeed – that we are dealing with complex relationships between subjectivities, but that this has to be carefully balanced by rigorously gathered and sensitively applied information concerning broader contexts – what might be commonly understood as 'objective' reality. Kress (1995: 90) shows a subtle awareness of the creative possibilities here:

> In a view of English as central in the making of a culture of innovation the production of subjectivity is at the centre, between social and cultural possibilities and forces on the one hand – available resources, structures of power – and the individual's action in the making of signs on the other . . . [the child's] interest in the making of signs may range from dispositions called 'conformity' to those called 'resistance' . . . Whether in solidarity or subversion, the child's own production of her representational resources is intimately connected, in a relation of reciprocity, with her production of her subjectivity.

This kind of formulation does, indeed, amount to a tough side of Romanticism, especially if we enlarge the illuminating focus to include the English teacher as well as the English taught. The author John Fowles has suggested something similar, furthering the connection between teaching and any artistic project:

> All artefacts please and teach the artist first, and other people later. The pleasing and teaching come from the explanation of self by the

expression of self; by seeing the self, and all the selves in the whole self, in the mirror of what the self created.

(Fowles 1981: 146)

This is not a justification for self-indulgence in teaching: far from it, it is, rather, an argument for pride in engagement with the noble profession. Unless the processes of teaching and learning may be seen in this sort of perspective, there is the distinct and very real danger that teachers – and by implication learners too – may become merely functionaries, alienated – in the Marxist sense to be explored later, and particularly with reference to ICT in Chapter 6 – from the essential nature of their activity.

Many in the teaching profession, in our experience, are acutely aware of this danger. Rex Gibson has characterised it as essentially 'a structure of feeling', although it clearly has its foundation in the realities of politically motivated educational legislation. If it is indeed a structure of feeling – like Blake's 'mind forg'd manacles' in his similarly radical critique of contemporary society, the poem *London* – it is all the more insidious and, therefore, dangerous. Structures of feeling tend to become deeply embedded, and take some shifting. Gibson went on to analyse this tendency as 'instrumental rationality'. As such, it

signifies a preoccupation with 'How to do it?' questions rather than with questions of 'Why do it?' or 'Where are we going?'. It is thus concerned with means rather than ends, with efficiency more than with consideration of purposes. In schools one manifestation is a stress on management and organisation at the expense of consideration of 'What is education for?'.

(Gibson 1984: 83)

All this amounts to a potentially disastrous, alienating and dichotomous separation of means and ends, of activity and purpose, with the process spawning its own dubious justification and particular – often impenetrable – rationality. Maybe all this sounds only too familiar for those professionally engaged in education, and this realisation can, itself, be rather debilitating. But, perhaps, precisely through a principled awareness of this precarious situation, there could be something far more positive at stake here: an awakened appreciation of the possibility of a new synthesis between the functional aspects of the subject English and its creative facets, based on a radical re-interpretation of the Romantic foundations of English teaching. Any such synthesis, however, has to be rigorously grounded in good practice and carefully reflective thought.

This is not to suggest that all we need to do to avoid the trap of instrumental rationality is to reconsider and clarify our original aims in the teaching of English. The relationship between means and ends is at once more complex, more subtle, and more potentially exciting than that. In practice, aims and activities inform and constantly modify each other, sometimes harmoniously, sometimes – rather more often, perhaps – in terms of struggle for coherent meaning-in-practice. The process is best seen as a dialectical one, with the meanings of teaching and learning constantly renewing themselves through praxis. Unavoidable in this context, as it determines the real possibilities of teaching and learning, is the culture of the classroom. As for other forms of culture, the term is complex and contentious, but its manifestations lie at the heart of English teaching. Many of the broader implications, especially along the lines of interculturality, will be explored subsequently. Some consideration, however, ought to take place right away – not least because it is often claimed by English teachers that the culture of the English classroom (the microcosmic notion of culture, in effect) is unlike that of any other subject classroom, and that English is fundamentally concerned with the transmission or mediation of particular models of culture (in its macrocosmic sense, ranging from notions of 'high culture' to multicultural ideas). As Eagleton has pointed out in his important consideration of the nature of culture (Eagleton 2000), the term is often considered in opposition to an equally complex, slippery term – 'nature' – which from this rather narrowly conceived 'cultural heritage' viewpoint may be likened to the pupils themselves.

So, underlying much of what is generally understood as education, especially in the particular context of schooling, is precisely this sort of binary opposition, where the raw material of the classroom – pupils in their untaught state, in effect – correspond to 'nature', to be modified – taught – by those representing, in some form or other, 'culture'. Eagleton, though, cuts into this all too familiar notion of culture, noting that

> Within this single term, questions of freedom and determinism, agency and endurance, change and identity, the given and the created, come dimly into focus. If culture means the active tending of natural growth, then it suggests a dialectic between the artificial and the natural, what we do to the world and what the world does to us. . . . So it is less a matter of deconstructing the opposition between culture and nature than of recognising that the term 'culture' is already such a deconstruction.
>
> (Eagleton 2000: 2)

As far as the English classroom is concerned, the matter is significant, and centres on notions of empowerment. Perhaps the cardinal rule of effective, adventurous English teaching is to recognise, develop and celebrate what is already there in the classroom, inevitably, as embodied in the linguistic experiences of everyone there (including, of course, the teacher) – and, by implication, many others not actually physically present at all but implied through influence. Conversely, the mistake so often made, not least in official pedagogical statements, is that teaching ought to start from some kind of clean slate. McGuinn takes up this point with reference to Bakhtin's 'authoritative texts' in Chapter 3. Eagleton's formulation of the complex relationship between culture and nature, rather than a simplistic opposition, is also relevant here, and is one we shall return to subsequently. Also relevant is the centrally Romantic notion of the validity of all experience, not simply that which is officially sanctioned in some sense or other. We do not need to go to child-centred pedagogical extremes to recognise that good teaching starts with what is there. In this it is similar to any other creative activity, and a good deal else besides.

Of all the Romantics, it is the insights of William Blake which I feel have most to say about the nature of education, and he is one of the guiding figures in this book's discussions. It seems to me that Blake alludes to a tension at the heart of the process of education no less now than in his own time. On the one hand we have the creative possibilities deriving from respect for youthful perceptions expressed in Blake's letter to his patron, the Reverend Trusler, in 1798: 'Neither youth nor childhood is folly or incapacity. Some children are fools and so are some old men. But there is a vast majority on the side of imagination or spiritual sensation'.

On the other hand, this sense of education as an opening out, carefully guided – taught, indeed – but ultimately relying on the autonomous activity of the learner, may be juxtaposed with Blake's awareness of the joyless, materialistic and deterministic approaches characteristic of the education processes around him. In particular, consider this description of the formal schooling of his day:

> But to go to school in a summer morn,
> Oh! It drives all joy away;
> Under a cruel eye outworn,
> The little ones spend the day
> In sighing and dismay.
>> (from 'The Schoolboy' in *Songs of*
>> *Innocence and of Experience*)

Matters have improved somewhat since Blake, himself largely unschooled, wrote this bleak description. And yet ... the stifling of the celebratory by means of initiative onslaught, intended or not; the strengthening of institutionalised education as a means of social control during the intervening two centuries – surely the tension remains powerfully apposite. Blake's value lies also in his own insistence that 'General knowledge is remote knowledge; it is in particulars that wisdom consists and happiness too' (from *Descriptive Catalogue* for *Vision of the Last Judgement*): a timely reminder that the focus needs to be what is actually possible in the classroom rather than on vague, general ideas. The point here is to notice, evaluate and either contest or develop the significance of the subtle nuances of the classroom and its culture. As Tripp (1993: 24–25) reminds us:

> The vast majority of critical incidents, however, are not at all dramatic or obvious: they are mostly straightforward accounts of very commonplace events that occur in routine professional practice which are critical in the . . . sense that they are indicative of underlying trends, motives and structures.

We shall be addressing Blake's 'particulars' throughout this book, illustratively and formatively: see, for example, McGuinn's analysis of his lesson on Tennyson's *Mariana* in Chapter 3, and my outline of teaching Dylan's *Subterranean Homesick Blues* later in the present chapter.

Blake's insistence on a clear, all-encompassing sense of direction is important too: such a sense informed his entire life's work. To return briefly to our initial questions – what are our overarching intentions in the classroom and beyond? What kind of education are we offering tomorrow's adult citizens? Questions like these address fundamental concerns about our future and, in that sense, any answers – even tentative ones – are essentially prophetic. Here, again, Blake is helpful: 'Every honest man', he declared, 'is a prophet; he utters his opinion both of private and public matters. Thus: if you go on so, the result is so. He never says, such a thing shall happen let you do what you will. A prophet is a seer, not an arbitrary dictator' (*Marginalia to Watson's Apology*). This formulation, as so often with Blake, gets to the heart of the matter: it is about empowerment, about what sort of life we want to see. And English teaching plays its part here, at a time when many people, teachers and pupils alike, see the future as somehow ordained by others – not even people sometimes, but faceless organisations. This is precisely what citizenship, especially as addressed in the English classroom, should be all about. Similarly, Blake's dictum that 'One law for the lion and the ox is oppression', appropriately included in his deliberately provocative *Proverbs of Hell*, addresses pertinently the issues of difference, of respect for subjectivity, and of the thorny problem of whether a mass education necessarily 'levels down' and too readily generalises. In this Blake prefigures such radical commentators on the nature of justice in education as Gale and Densmore:

> The proposal that adopting uniform standards for teaching and learning will automatically result in academic success is challenged by an inclusive discourse of difference that views formal education as perpetuating pedagogical practices and which impede academic growth of certain groups of students in ways that most people do not seem to recognise.
>
> (Gale and Densmore 2000: 123)

Precisely in order to achieve this elusive recognition, English may play a decisive role. Diverse textual readings and the creation of wide-ranging artefacts, fostering simultaneous breadth and depth in meaning-making, are fundamental to successful and adventurous English teaching. Few would disagree with this statement, but the implications are, in fact, huge. We intend to explore in this book some of these possibilities in practical and theoretical terms, especially in their relationship to the current structure of the English curriculum. There is good cause to celebrate the diversity of texts available for study and creation in the English classroom, whether as separate entities or in inter-textual combinations: media, ICT, political and intercultural contexts all invite exciting, if simultaneously complex and demanding, teaching and learning. Again, McGuinn's later exposition of the implications of Bakhtin's 'authoritative texts' for English teachers, in Chapter 3, is highly pertinent.

So, too, is the teaching of literature generally, and its centrality in the English curriculum is, for us, something well worth fighting for – certainly not in opposition, or as hierarchically superior, to other dimensions of English teaching but, rather, in dynamic relationship with them. Further, whereas a great deal of writing about English literature teaching has focused on its empathetic possibilities – how it *feels* to be of another culture in terms of time, place or class, for instance – we intend here also to explore ways in which literature may be taught as a more personally (but also radically) liberating force: a rediscovery of innocence; a sense of wonder, and of strangeness: Bruner's telling formulation 'violation of expectancy' springs to mind here. Literature in this context may be seen to carry fundamentally aesthetic as well as social connotations and, for this reason, its study is as much an arts-based as a humanities-based subject, insofar as this distinction is helpful. The uses of literature in teaching are at once profoundly intense and enormously wide-ranging. As the novelist Aidan Chambers maintains:

> I would go as far as to say that it is this particular use of language – the literary use that some have called 'storying' – that defines humanity and makes us human. . . . this particular form of language and our skill in using it empower us in being what we are, and make it possible for us to conceive of being more than we are.
>
> (Chambers 1985: 2–3)

The author Anne Fine echoed this perception in her (unpublished) speech to the National Association for the Teaching of English (NATE) (North East) Conference in June 2002, defending the empathic relevance of imaginative fiction: 'People who can't understand how others tick are impoverished.' The possibilities for inter-textual, social and aesthetic combinations of experience and insight are exciting – indeed, they characterise much of the best English teaching in practice. C. S. Lewis, whose magical-realist writing certainly awakened many children's and adults' eyes to the possibilities of wonder, has reminded us, 'through literature I become a thousand people and yet remain myself' (in Chambers 1985: 5).

Literature teaching – especially, perhaps, when experiencing poetry – has this vast, magical potential; and it is not merely a matter of extending empathy, important though this is, but of awakening to the wonder of any experience, even when culturally denoted as trivial. This is important, for in our celebrity-obsessed world it is all too easy to be gulled into thinking that real life exists somewhere else. There is an implication here for media education within English: the sense that with ever-increasing media sophistication in the creation of virtual realities on the one hand, and a tendency to dehumanise language into soundbites on the other, it is all the more important to deconstruct the resulting texts and their means of transmission. There is also an implication for literature, in that there may be a means here of creating, through the conscious use of crafted language, both meaning (critical, questioning) *and* celebration (magical, convivial) out of everyday experience. Neil Astley, in the introduction to his vibrant poetry anthology 'Staying Alive' maintains that

> sensitivity to language is what distinguishes us as civilised people, both as human beings and as individuals, registering our intelligence as well as our alertness and attention to the lives of others. A poem lives in its language, which is body to its soul. Joseph Brodsky believed that our purpose in life as human beings was 'to create civilisation', and that 'poetry is essentially the soul's search for its release in language'.
>
> (Astley 2002: 21)

The poet Simon Armitage, much read in the 14–16 English classroom, manages to remind us of both in his poem *That feeling, I mean*. In this and in many others of his poems, he offers the sort of insight which should resonate with the experience of English teachers as it does with ours: the sense that value and meaning is potentially available in the classroom. If our years of teaching English in a wide range of schools, and of visiting many more English classrooms in the context of teacher education, have taught us anything, it is that this wealth of experience and insight is always there. We should never be surprised, and yet frequently we are (in the best possible way), by these riches. In this respect the teaching of English is a thoroughly artistic endeavour, in the sense that Raymond Williams suggested: 'To communicate through the arts is to convey an experience to others in such a form that the experience is actively recreated, actively lived through by those to whom it is offered' (in NACCCE 1999: 70).

A great part of the skill of teaching English lies in fostering the appropriate culture of the classroom to give credibility to students' insights and experiences, and in making creative connections with and between them. This is not to suggest that the purpose of teaching English is simply to enable, in a passive sense: we are back to the 'tougher side of the Romantic movement' here. The skill of the English teacher lies in stimulating the recollection of such experience – in tranquillity or otherwise – and in listening intently to the voices of the classroom in order that genuine meaning-making may occur. Whatever the content of the lesson itself, whether it be prescribed or not, whether it be obviously 'creative' or not, effective English teaching starts from what is there. The teacher's repertoire has then to include the ability to take this further, making inter-textual and intercultural connections as appropriate, either towards planned and pre-stated learning objectives or, if necessary, being guided by the tone of the lesson towards uncharted territory.

In practice, most lessons are something of a mixture of the planned and the spontaneous, and many would say that the opportunities for the latter have dwindled catastrophically in the context of an overcrowded curriculum and increasing insistence on detailed planning with clearly stated lesson objectives. The point here is that planning and clear objectives are important aspects of teaching – but then so is the cultivation of a sense of adventure in learning and reflection on experience, and it takes a certain degree of courage to acknowledge this in practice, perhaps for both teacher *and* pupils. There may be an illuminating parallel here between the teacher's and the novelist's art: to be successful, the openings, especially, of either a school lesson or a novel must both disclose and withhold information. It's a skilfully implemented balancing act; if too much is withheld, either deliberately or accidentally, the project may simply be confusing; if too little, there is little sense of the unpredictable or adventurous – the learners may simply switch off, or the novel readers discard the book. If the novel's being read in an English lesson, of course, both may happen – and I can think of at least one instance of this in my (distant!) experience. Perhaps it is best to envisage the learning objectives as both clear *and* open-ended – less of the 'by the end of this lesson you will have learned that . . .' (after all who are we to dictate to thirty or so adolescents exactly what will go through their heads over an hour or so in the classroom?) and more a sense of 'by the end of this lesson you will have had the opportunity to discover, explore and learn about . . .'.

The nature of this kind of tension, between pre-ordained aims and the need for genuine exploration, will be considered further in relation to practice later in this chapter and elsewhere – in McGuinn's study of ICT in English teaching (Chapter 5), for example. Clearly, there are other tensions involved too, which may have more to do with the fostered culture of the classroom, less to do with the intricacies of lesson planning – although, of, course the two are inextricably and influentially linked. It may be helpful here to borrow from, and adapt for English teaching, C. K. Stead's insight into the nature of poetic creation. For Stead (1964: 11):

> A poem may be said to exist in a triangle, the points of which are: first, the poet; second, the audience; and, third, the areas of experience which we call variously 'Reality', 'Truth', or 'Nature'. Between these points run lines of tension, and depending on the time, the place, the poet, and the audience, these lines will lengthen or shorten . . . There are infinite variations, but . . . the finest poems are likely to be those which exist in an equilateral triangle, each point pulling equally in a moment of perfect tension.

Stead developed his thesis through a close reading of several poets, but it strikes me that there is pointed relevance here to the process of English teaching.

Reflecting on this connection, I wrote in a previous context (Fleming and Stevens 1998: 5) of the dynamic possibilities:

> A great deal depends on what goes into the triangle, and what exactly is represented by each of the three points. If we take the triangle to enclose and express the whole business of English teaching, which, like Stead's poem, is *created*, then it may follow that one point represents the English teacher; another, the audience of pupils (although this may not be the only possible audience); and the final point symbolises the context – the outer world, perhaps, which exerts so many often contra-dictory pressures on the process of teaching. . . . effective teaching depends on the maintenance of a certain tension along the lines joining the points: if the points become too close to, or too distant from, either each other or the central project of teaching itself, there may well be a danger that the creative art of teaching could be damaged. This is in the end an argument for a dynamic combination of reflective distance and imaginative involvement – qualities which may seem like opposites, and perhaps they are; but to go back to Blake's *Marriage of Heaven and Hell*, 'Without contraries is no progression'.

It may seem something of a paradox, but effective English teaching along these broad lines needs to be both rigorous in creating the objective circum-stances for the essential security of the classroom to be established, and open minded so that subjective experience may blossom. A Zen koan expresses a similarly pointed paradox: the way to control a flock of sheep is to provide a wide enough pasture for them to wander (wonder?) in. For the shepherd/teacher (embodying the pastoral essence of teaching) such a project involves boundary maintenance, fertilising the ground, and tending the creatures themselves, as well as simply providing the space – all important considerations in developing the tensions of the classroom triangle.

Good practice in this context may well be liberating, for students and teachers alike, based as it is on attentiveness to how young people learn through engagement in meaningful activity and reflection. Isca Salzberger-Wittenberg presents this state of alertness as central to any effective teaching, and so it is: 'What is needed *in the first place* is the willingness to pay attention; to listen and look and use all our senses to apprehend what is being communicated' (Salzberger-Wittenberg *et al.* 1983: 61, my italics).

Harrison (1994: 7) expressed this mission through the apt metaphor of the theatre, asking:

> Could the theatre of education . . . be trying too hard to 'deliver the goods' to its clients, the learners, and leaving no space for them to develop their own vision? Are we providing enough space for learners to bring their own minds and cultures into taking part in learning? Have we lost sight of essential qualities such as play, curiosity and friendship in learning? Whose production *is* it anyway?

Whose indeed? To answer the question affirmatively through the act of teaching is to be able at times to live with a Keatsian 'negative capability': 'that is when man is capable of being in uncertainties, mysteries, doubts without any irritable reaching after fact and reason'. In this sense, teaching is, indeed, an art, and the implications of the vitally essential attentiveness will be further explored throughout this book. As will those of William Blake's pertinent observation warning against lazy, unalert perception:

> We are led to believe a lie
> When we see not through the eye
>   (from *Auguries of Innocence*)

It is, indeed, a matter of perception, and it is basic. de Bono realised that:

> If our perceptions are wrong then no amount of logical excellence will give the right answer. So it is a pity that almost the whole of our traditional intellectual effort has been directed at logic and so little at perception. Logic will not change emotions and feelings. Perception will.
>   (de Bono 1996: 248)

And, as we aim to show in this book, it is possible – indeed essential – to make positive use of the English curriculum, with all its constraints and overcrowding, as the means of achieving the kind of classroom that is conducive to meaningful perception.

The term 'meaningful perception' implies just that: perception that is full of meaning. Precisely whose meaning is another matter, but, inevitably, it too is inextricably tied up in the culture of the classroom. Clearly, meaning is not a neutral substance, waiting to be discovered; neither is it tenable to allow any meaning to become as valid as any other. But as a stage in the process of meaning-making, it is often advisable to allow tentative, exploratory freedom for investigation and creation, intervening as teacher with both sensitivity and critical awareness. This is the essence of critical literacy as it may be – and frequently is, in our experience – practised in the classroom. By its very nature, such a process is subversive of existing power structures, including those generally characteristic of the classroom, and it is – potentially at least – empowering. Lankshear (1997: 78) endorses this empowerment in terms of literacy, an area absolutely central, clearly, to the project of English teaching:

> The powerfully literate reader can contest texts, resisting meanings and positions these would otherwise 'impose'. . . . As a writer of texts the powerfully literate person develops 'powerful competencies' with a range of genres and techniques which may be employed in pursuit of personal, ethical and political purposes.

Significantly, Lankshear alludes to both reading and writing in this context, whereas for many in education, and outside it, the term 'literacy' applies principally to reading only. Writing is, in fact, vitally important here – in the broadest sense of the word as making all kinds of texts, thereby experimenting with both form and meaning. Monaghan and Saul (in Green 1993: 202) distinguish writing in schools from reading, characterising the former, potentially at least, as the more active:

> However variously reading and writing have been defined, it still remains the case that reading, even when oral, is the receptive skill . . . while writing is the productive skill. The distinction is relevant when the question of control is considered. The curriculum is, at least in part, the formal statement of what society believes it is important for students to know. Society has focused on children as readers because, historically, it has been much more interested in children as receptors rather than producers of the written word.

Many would question whether it is entirely apt to view reading primarily as a receptive skill, but writing is, without a doubt, a potentially liberating, active force.

The reality of writing in the classroom, however – and the English classroom certainly does not escape this observation – is all too often defined by drudgery and pointlessness. Or if there is a point, it is frequently, implicitly or explicitly, one of classroom control. The central tension concerning the role of writing in school is inescapable: a means of control inflicted on a more or less unwilling student population, as against a creative and critically empowering means of expression. Surely it must be one of the defining purposes of English teaching to promote the latter at the expense of the former, as is illustrated by McGuinn in Chapter 4 with reference to his Malaysian pupil. A further case in point from recent experience: a Year 10 student (age 15) was reprimanded by his German teacher for laughing while his classmate was being told off, and then told to write his version of the incident. This is what he came up with:

Laughter

I did not mean to find anything funny. I think I must have been rather depressed beforehand (the war, the world etc etc) [it was the time of the invasion of Iraq] and therefore found it quite necessary to relieve myself (of my current state of depression) by having a fit of laughter in which I found great joy and managed to vanquish any knights of evil depression from the grounds of my castle. I now find myself quite rejuvenated and, in the words of my good friend George Orwell, 'laughter breeds happiness'.

The End.

For writing this the student in question was given another detention, during which he was told to write out large chunks of the school rules, thus implying that writing is inherently a painful process appropriate as a mundane punishment. The point is not, of course, to endorse any undermining of discipline for teachers under pressure in their classroom control; rather to question the nature of possible responses to this kind of incident. Schools – English teachers especially – need to find ways to celebrate writing such as this, sophisticated, reflective and contextualised as it is, without getting bogged down in rules and punishments. Incidents like this, potentially, have great bearing on the cultures of classrooms. The opening of Jennifer Johnston's novel *Shadows on our Skin* (1987: 7–8), although set rather differently in the Northern Ireland Troubles, makes and illustrates a similar point. The main protagonist, a school student called Joseph Logan, writing poetry about his absent father during a maths lesson on the equilateral triangle (perhaps particularly apt in the light of C. K. Stead's

13. /9/99   Kyle.

~~XXXX~~ me!

Favourites.
1. tv.
2. Music

Kyle's split knee.

Hello, my name Kyle moore. I'm here because
my English teacher gave me the choice of
talking about my Fantastik Favourites
or a totally crazy disturbing story about an
event in my life so this ^here I go with my choice.
"Mum I dont wont a bath" I cried, "I wont to go
play on the garage roffe ^roof with le and
fred" Now can I please?".
"No you b##XX+g well cant. Now get
up there and take this with you. Mum gave
me a glass up to take to the ^know
bath. Being only six I dident No the
danger of glass. I gazed at the bath
steming like hot lava (Why did mum
insist ~~me~~ I have a red hot bath?) I said
to myself forgeting the mud on my head
and the smell of my feet. I got in.
yowWWWWWW W W WWW w w www
"I was melting" "god save me" I ~~utterd~~.
                                        uttered

"ahhh thats better" I said to my self standing up in the bathe with my glass cup. Open, I Jumped! It was my sister but I really did Jump and Landed on the glass– cup knee first. No sooner had I landed but the bathe turned red.

I will not continue because those I started acting babyish

part two. Kyle's Split Knee. Sponsored by me.

"Wahhh wahhh wahhh" my mum I ust stared at me like a zombie. "mum I'm bleeeeding" I cried. Duuuuuuuuu (Hmm She has a problem) I thought, launching myself out of the bath. I hopped Round the house intil my Dad tackled Rugby tackled me to the floor. "Kyle! the more you cry the more youll bleed". Whaaaaa (I would be better used as an intruder alarm) Then man I blacked out. When I awoke I heard a and my Dad talking. Then I noticed I was in a hospital bed. After a while a doctor and my parents came in and the doctor said "I am DODDoctor staaaaanly IIm a...ffrad yowe cut your leggg open." then he had to thrust off and my dad said con my mum "I DDDont ttrust hummmm." Theres hot much MORE I can tell you apart from the stitches ~~stitchs~~ ~~hurt~~ lick h**# and I got a sweet.

so. good day all you good people and so long.

The End.

229 77

Kyle's Split Knee   sponserd by me!

Hello my names kyle. Im here because my English teacher gave me the choice of talking about my fantastic favourite or a totally crazy disgusting story about an event in my life so hire I go with my choice.

'Mum I dont wont a bath' I cried, 'I wont to go play on the garage roff with lee and fred Now can I please.'

'No you b*****y well cant. Now get up there and take this with you.' Mum gave me a glass cup to take to the bath. being only six I dident No the danger of glass. I gazed at the bath steming like hot lava (why did mum insist I have a red hot bath?) I said to myself forgeting the mud on my head and the smell of my feet. I got in. yowwwwwwwWWWWWWwwwww I was melting 'god save me' I utterd. 'ahhh thats better' I said to my self standing in the batho with my glass cup. Open, I jumped! It was my sister but I really did jump and landed on the glass knee first. No sooner had I landed but the bathe turned red.

I will not continue because I started acting babyish

Part two. Kyle's split knee. Sponserd by me!

'Wahhh wahhh wahhh' My mum just stared at me like a zombie. 'mum Im bleeeeding' I cried. Duuuuuuuuu (Husten she has a problem) I thoute, launching myself out of the bath. I hoped Round the house intil my dad Rugby takeld me to the floor. 'Kyle! The more you cry the more youll bleed'. Whaaaa (I would be better yoused as an intruder alarm) Then I blaked out. When I awoke I heard a man and my dad talking. Then I noticed I was in a hospital bed. After a wile a doctor and my perence came in and the doctor said 'I am DDDDoctor Staaaaanly IIm a . . . ffrad you've cut your leggg open'. Then he had to rush off and my dad said to my mum 'I DDDont ttrust himmmm.' Theres not much more I can tell you apart from the stichis hert lick h*** and I got a sweet.

> So good day all you
>
> Good people and so long.
>
> The End.

poem-in-a-triangle cited above), is severely upbraided by his teacher for inattentiveness: 'If I had my way I would open that door, and let you and all the others who don't wish to learn go home and wallow in your ignorance. Wallow.'

Consider a further example of a pupil's writing – in this instance officially validated as a piece of English curricular work – undertaken by a Year 7 (11 year old) in his first couple of weeks at secondary school by way of an introductory task set for the whole class. There is certainly nothing especially noteworthy in the English teacher's setting of the assignment – to write about a favourite pastime, or about an autobiographical incident – as a way of judging pupils' standards of writing and simultaneously learning a little about them relatively early in the teacher–pupil relationship. But the resulting piece of writing has much to teach us nevertheless. It is presented here in full, starting on p. 16, initially in the original hand-written form (before any teacher-inserted corrections) and then as typescript.

'The best writing is vigorous, committed, honest and interesting', wrote Cox, famously, in the prelude to the first version of the National Curriculum for English (DES 1989) – before equally famously deciding, with his committee, that such qualities could not be fitted in to the imposed structure of the curriculum being formed. English teachers generally would no doubt agree that this writing positively displays these characteristics in abundance, along with many others. Interestingly, this piece of writing arose not from particularly creative teaching – although in more general terms the culture of the English classroom as established allowed, even encouraged, this sort of personal writing – but from a pretty standard task. Rather, it may well be in the teacher's possible response to the work that there would be an opportunity for creative approaches. Certainly 'Kyle's Split Knee' displays many positive qualities: it is both thoroughly engaged and engaging, and there is a sophisticated awareness of both readership (and its possible interpretations) and the role of the author (occasionally standing aside from the narrative flow). It has, too, an innovative awareness of the forms of narrative writing, to the point of playful subversion, while some of the vocabulary and expressive language is both inventive and mature. Further, there is a pleasing balance between dialogue and narrative/descriptive passages, economically hinting at broader realities (even quite disturbing ones) in the best traditions of short story writing as the story is driven along energetically. Ultimately there is a celebratory delight in language, evident throughout but perhaps particularly noticeable in the description of the doctor's language and in Kyle's father's reactions to it. Doubtless there are many other impressive qualities, uncoverable through a careful, sympathetic reading. However, all these points notwithstanding, the faults of the piece in terms of spelling and occasional punctuation lapses would prevent it being awarded more than a level

3 in National Curriculum terms, and more likely it would end up (as indeed it did) with a level 2. Such a response, if made clear to the pupil – and there is an issue here about entitlement and transparency of assessment – runs the risk of being thoroughly demotivating. The teacher is, indeed, caught here, wishing to celebrate achievement while simultaneously recognising the need to improve the presentational aspects of this pupil's writing. The situation will be familiar to all those involved in English teaching. The further problem is that re-drafting and meticulous proof reading are unlikely to appeal to the pupil in question – it is the vivid freshness of the writing that is one of its most attractive features, as much for the writer as for the reader. One possible creative response to such work might be to suggest to the writer that his work is of such value that it could be displayed in the classroom (or included in some sort of anthology) as an example of good practice, and that in order for this to happen it ought to be re-presented in word-processed, even illustrated, form. Even this may not work, but at least it accentuates the celebratory and audience-oriented aspects of the work, as well as appealing to the possibilities of creative, integrated uses of ICT. I will discuss more fully the nature of creative teaching and learning in the next chapter, and McGuinn will take up some of the ICT-related implications in Chapter 5.

Examples such as these and others cited throughout this book serve, I hope, to give a fuller flavour of some of the kinds of writing habitually created in schools. They also show how important it is to emphasise meaning-making in the context of writing, through the development of Lankshear's 'powerful competencies', as there is a very real danger that teaching students to become adept in 'a range of genres and techniques' without questioning their purposes and potential meanings could mean that we fall into the trap of perpetuating instrumental rationality as discussed previously. McGuinn explores this critique of the place of genre theory in English teaching more fully in Chapter 4. To teach emulation of generic characteristics and conventions, however perceptive or expert, is, in the end, meaningless – literally – unless predicated on a critical exploration of latent and explicit meanings. Take, for example, that stock in trade of the English classroom, the study and subsequent construction of magazine advertisements. Marvellous work can be, and frequently is, done here – colourful, vibrant, and (given ICT availability) semi-professional productions. But without focused critical exploration of meaning and purpose – ultimately ethical and political as well as formal questions – these productions remain empty attempts at emulation of an unchallenged, power-based form of literacy. Worse than meaningless, in effect, they encourage replication of the very power structures and their attendant literacies which are likely most to exploit passive, unquestioning reading. The nature of the writing undertaken, then, is inextricably linked – and reflects back into – the possible modes of reading.

The themes touched on in this opening chapter will be returned to in greater detail subsequently. Two areas in particular deserve special attention. The first is concerned with notions of culture and its various relationships to English teaching and learning, and to creativity in general. This strand culminates in an exploration of the nature of the intercultural classroom as the model that best meets the needs of English teaching for the twenty-first century. The second area, closely related, focuses on critical literacy and the twin concerns for empathetic engagement and distanced evaluation. For now, however, it is time to explore in rather greater depth and detail the 'minute particulars' Blake referred to as preferable to 'remote knowledge'; in other words, the vivid reality of English as it may be taught.

Mention has already been made of the contentious issue of lesson aims and objectives – contentious in that it raises questions of transparency in teaching and learning through explicit intentions (clearly a 'good thing') and, rather more dubiously, questions of narrowness in lesson/scheme of work objectives implying a curriculum-delivery mode of teaching. For the following illustrative sequences of English classroom practice, a certain structural pattern has been adopted in order to facilitate the kind of culture of creative learning endorsed in this book. Broadly, and rather more descriptively than prescriptively, the pattern involves three stages: first, an exploratory stage, during which reactions to a given stimulus or theme are tentatively elicited and offered; then, second, a phase involving rather more carefully negotiated meaning, focused on various possibilities for understanding, interpretation and broader contextual exploration; and finally, the making, sharing and critical evaluation of artefacts as appropriate. Stated, and if possible negotiated, objectives would need to correspond to this shape and would require continuing pointed reference throughout the teaching and learning processes. The teacher's role is varied – at first stimulating a broad range of responses, opening up to learners' experiences and perceptions, and providing the necessary texts and contexts to encourage their expression. Then the development of a phase of 'intensification' of meaning through rigorous questioning and negotiation and, if appropriate, the judicious introduction of further resources to stimulate deeper thought. I have found it helpful here to compare such a process to the musical development of a symphony (or, conceivably, another art form): tentative exploration of thematic possibilities through trial and error following a captivating opening, subsequently giving way to intensification of a particular theme or motif. Clearly, the range of symphonic expression is as vast as the possibilities for successful, invigorating English lessons, so we need not fear constraint through this parallel. Critical evaluation, pertinent reflection and celebratory creativity all have a part to play throughout the sequence of activities – which may span one or more lessons, depending on the nature of the teaching and learning taking place. However, some kind of combination of the three has a particular role as the culmination of the period of study. Again, the similarity to the symphonic form seems to me striking, with meditative reflection or joyous celebration through thematic synthesis the obvious possible climaxes. The four-part or three-part lesson structures so beloved of the National Strategy: English Strand (optional starter – introduction – development – plenary), it may be seen, could very easily co-exist with the structure suggested here – although experience shows that a starter activity is most effective when linked to the rest of the learning.

The first illustration comprises a three-lesson sequence focusing on three contrasting texts' portrayals of advice to the young – a subject eminently suitable for the English curriculum, and with added relevance to citizenship education – taught to a mixed-ability group of Year 10 pupils (aged 14–15) in a comprehensive school. By way of introduction, in the light of the comments made above concerning the nature of lesson openings, we read and discussed – briefly – Heaney's poem *Digging*. This was very much an introductory activity – even a starter – with three publicly stated purposes: first, raising the class's awareness of the potent possibilities of poetic language; second, introducing orally the theme of the expectations adults have of the young and how the latter respond; and, third, playing with the central metaphor of 'digging', with some discussion of the semantic field of this word, including the 1960's 'hip' connotation of enjoyment and/or understanding (a meaning most of the group were surprisingly familiar with).

From this opening, the class went on to consider three contrasting but thematically linked texts: Bob Dylan's 1965 classic *Subterranean Home-sick Blues*, an extract from *Hamlet* in which Polonius gives fatherly advice to his departing son Laertes, and an extract from a contemporary American website offering guidance to the young. The latter two of these are included below; the lyrics to the Dylan song may be found in his compilation *Lyrics 1962–1965* (1985), and the song itself is on the 1965 album *Bringing It All Back Home* and on the video of the 1965 Pennebaker film *Don't Look Back*.

The sequence of activities proceeded as follows:

1   A three-stage reading and exploration of *Subterranean Homesick Blues*: first, as a written text only, read aloud with copies for each student; second, through listening to the recording; and, finally, through watching the video clip in which Dylan stands nonchalantly leafing through and discarding placards depicting key words and phrases – the opening of the 1965 Pennebaker film *Don't Look Back*. The readings and discussions considered how each layer, or 'framing', of the text altered and modified possible interpretations, with written, sung and visual elements complementing each other, and how the text relates to the theme of adult advice to the young.

2   Particular poetic/playful elements of the text were explored and re-presented by small groups, focusing on given sections. Notable here were points made about 'manhole/man whole', 'success/suck cess', 'dig yourself', 'twenty years of schooling' and 'the day shift', and 'you don't need a weather man to know which way the wind blows'. The general subversion of adult advice disdainfully running through the text, alongside the possibility of a different way of living ('manhole/man whole', 'success/suck cess'), was appreciated – by some in the group, in any case – and various connections made to more contemporary songs dealing with similar issues.

From *Hamlet*: Polonius (to his son Laertes, about to leave for university in France):

And these few precepts in thy memory
Look thou character. Give thy thoughts no tongue,
Nor any unproportioned thought his act.
Be thou familiar, but by no means vulgar.
Those friends thou hast, and their adoption tried,
Grapple them unto thy soul with hoops of steel,
But do not dull thy palm with entertainment
Of each new-hatched unfledged courage. Beware
Of entrance to a quarrel; but being in,
Bear't that th' opposed may beware of thee.
Give every man thine ear, but few thy voice;
Take each man's censure, but reserve thy judgement.
Costly thy habit as thy purse can buy,
But not expressed in fancy; rich, not gaudy,
For the apparel oft proclaims the man,
And they in France of the best rank and station
Are of a most select and generous chief in that.
Neither a borrower nor a lender be,
For loan oft loses both itself and friend,
And borrowing dulleth edge of husbandry.
This above all, to thine own self be true,
And it must follow as the night the day
Thou canst not then be false to any man.

(Act 1, Scene 3, ll. 58–80)

From an American website offering advice to adolescents:

Cultural influences

If you experience restrictive socialization practices that emphasize family values (i.e., you are residing in a collectivist culture and/or experience narrow socialization):

Dear 'narrowly-socialized' adolescent,
   Although you may feel you lack control over your life and constantly answer to a higher authority, let me assure you that there is still hope. In fact, it is most likely to your advantage that your parents value discipline and respect. You will eventually reach an age when you will become completely independent. You may realize then that your parents' intentions lied in your benefit. Be grateful that you have someone who cares for you!
   I believe that you need people in your life to have a fulfilled life. People – parents, friends, peers – are most important during adolescence. You look for advice and you give advice. You need restraints to have discipline and to understand and respect others. As you get older, you will be thankful for these restraints. I grew up in an Italian Catholic family and I am grateful for all of the rules because now I have such great respect . . . Just keep an open mind and talk to your parents. Don't shut them out. Well, being that I was brought up in a collectivist society as well, I am pretty sure that I know what you are going through. But, if you think that they do not respect or care about you, then you are wrong. Try to understand why your family acts the way they do. . . . when you get older your parents will lighten up.
   . . . I know it is rough to have parents that are really strict when you are trying to find yourself. My advice to you is to try to talk to your parents about ways in which you can express yourself without them freaking out. Maybe they will allow you to take baby steps towards becoming the individual they know you will become. The age that you are now approaching is hard on you as well as your parents because they have to learn that they need to let go. This is hard because you are their child and they will always see you like this. Give it a little time and they will come around.
   (www.crab.rutgers.edu/~chmarkey/adviceforadolescents.htm)

3   At this point, two lessons into the sequence, the group were introduced
    to the extract from *Hamlet*, a volunteer reading Laertes while the
    teacher read the part of Polonius and provided a brief context for the
    scene. Subsequent discussion perceived both validity and hypocrisy in
    Polonius' advice, and, having carefully interpreted the words, groups
    of three experimented with different ways of handling the scene with
    the emphasis on contrasting attitudes shown by Laertes and the silent
    Ophelia to their father's advice.

4   The next activity combined elements of the two texts, with groups
    preparing and performing the Polonius speech in the manner of the
    Dylan performance, providing a rhythmic sense of the verse, and
    discarding placards displaying the chosen key words and phrases. As a
    pop video there is much to be said for choosing to emulate something
    which is both straightforward to enact and produce, unlike the slick
    MTV varieties, and is outside young people's usual repertoire. Some of
    the results were startlingly effective.

5   The next stage involved students' research into appropriate texts
    dealing with the theme of adults' advice, from a wide range of sources
    and relating to notions of citizenship. Each group took two or three
    examples and presented them to the rest of the class as the basis for
    further discussion. The website example, provided by the teacher as a
    further resource, was used and analysed as an example – eliciting
    various responses from some who felt it made good sense to others who
    regarded it as patronising or vacuous or both.

6   The final activity, four lessons in, was to create a meaningful expres-
    sion of dialogue between adults and young people, choosing the
    medium that suited each group best. Extracts from each of the three
    texts could be, and were, used, alongside students' own expressions.
    Poetry, song, mime and letter-writing were all successfully represented
    in a celebratory finale.

Of course, this bald summary does scant justice to the richness of the
experience for all concerned, in terms both of critical understanding of texts
and creative modelling. It may, however, serve as some sort of prompt to
suggest how inter-textual connections may be made and re-made in a
context of vital engagement, as indeed is McGuinn's description in Chapter
4 of how an English teacher might analyse a text written on the side of a
rice packet. The possibilities for adaptation and extension are infinite: it's
a fertile theme. One conceivable adaptation could be as a starting point for
A/AS level study of *Hamlet*. An underlying theme of both these resource
materials and the play itself – after all, the play's the thing – is the distinction between appearance and reality; the perception about who exactly in
a duplicitous world may be trustworthy: 'seems, madam? Nay it is. I know
not seems.' One student, illustrating on his placard the final words quoted

from Polonius' speech to Laertes, chose to highlight just one word: 'False' – uncannily apt in the light of Polonius's subsequent devious, untrusting and manipulative behaviour towards both his son and daughter.

Indeed, perhaps the most fitting testimony to the students' ideas and verve is in my own seeing of a familiar text in new ways. Kierkegaard's insistence that 'to be a teacher in the right sense is to be a learner. I am not a teacher, only a fellow student' might seem a little disingenuous, but at times it rings true – especially in the openness to experience characteristic of a creatively oriented classroom. I refer here to the Dylan song and its performance, which yielded riches that even I, as a long-standing and ardent Dylan admirer, had not expected. For instance, one pupil pointed out that Dylan's reference to the vacuous 'day shift', the reward for 'twenty years schooling', is mirrored and accentuated in his style of delivery in the film version: seemingly bored by the meaningless, repetitive nature of his action in discarding the placards in turn. This sort of perception brings to mind two quotations from quite different sources. The first, from the Key Stage Three Strategy (DfEE 2001: 10), behoves teachers to encourage literacy that is 'sensitive to the ways meanings are made', and 'reflective, critical, discriminatory'. The second refers to a comment made by the poet Liz Lochead (NATE North East Conference 21/6/03) insisting that 'the poem should teach the reader how to read it'. It seems significant that teaching and learning of this kind may satisfy such contrasting sets of criteria: exactly the challenge English teachers need to meet and resolve.

2 Romantically linked

Notions of creativity

[A] small water-insect on the surface of rivulets . . . *wins* its way up against the stream, by alternate pulses of active and passive motion, now resisting the current, and now yielding to it in order to gather strength and a momentary *fulcrum* for a further propulsion. This is no unapt emblem of the mind's self-experience in the act of thinking.

(Samuel Taylor Coleridge, from *Biographia Literaria*)

There is something – many things perhaps – especially challenging about the subject English. I mean this in at least two senses. Teaching the subject is certainly a challenge for its practitioners, given its tensions, breadth and sometimes tenuous purposes, some of which have already been touched upon. More significantly in the present context it may be that, in fulfilling some of its purposes and resolving a few of the tensions, the dynamic teaching of English poses a challenge to the status quo. After all, ultimately, English deals in and with words, antithetical to the silence demanded by oppression in its various guises; as Kureishi has pointed out in an illuminating essay: 'Tyrants are involved with silence as a form of control. Who says what to whom, and about what, is of compelling interest to authorities, to dictators, fathers, teachers, and officials of whichever type' (2003: 4).

Pejorative mention of teachers (and fathers) notwithstanding, it is the sense of English as implying radical intentions that will be the basis of this chapter – although, of course, seeing and practising the teaching of English in this way is, in itself, quite a challenge. There is also a sense that English, relatively unburdened by a huge body of information to transmit to its pupils, may be more free to focus on the nature of understanding and insight as the basis of knowledge; the danger otherwise, in Saul Bellow's pithy phrase, is that: 'We are informed about everything, but we know nothing' (in Nobel 1996: 125). This is especially relevant in the context of the 'information-rich age' we are frequently said to be living in, and is examined more closely by McGuinn in Chapter 5 in terms of the implications of ICT.

So, as Brindley (1994: 11) puts it:

> English has a special power to challenge conventions, institutions, governments, business interests – any established system. This resides in the fact that English is concerned with the uncontrollable power of a shared language that we all speak and the uncontrollable responses to what we read. The work of English teaching involves continual pressing for the expression of alternative ideas, inviting challenge to received opinions, seeking strong personal responses, establishing debate.

This is quite a claim and, of course, it was written before the more recent initiatives and stipulations have, in the eyes of some, rather narrowed the radical potential of the subject. Our challenges as English teachers are, first of all, to verify this kind of claim, and then to consider exactly what the radical implications may be in practice. And the twin ideas I should like to propose as crucial to the argument are those associated with creativity on the one hand, and those related to the intercultural dimension on the other. Nobel (1996: 28) poses the fundamental question to be addressed from a Steinerian perspective, having previously drawn on physiological insights into the dangerous neglect of the human brain's creative potential. Her question is certainly pertinent: 'Might it be that the very nature of our system of education leads to our becoming, from a physiological point of view, "mechanised in the mind" and less capable of grasping whole contexts?'

The notion of creativity, especially as pertaining to the teaching of English, is notoriously complex. Not least this may be because all English teachers, in my experience, like to feel that their craft is, in some way or another, creative – even if, or perhaps especially when, there are external constraints on creative practice. There is something of an urgent imperative for schools to fit themselves for the (post-)modern world; Hargreaves makes the point that:

> It is plain that if teachers do not acquire and display this capacity to redefine their skills for the task of teaching, and if they do not model in their own conduct the very qualities – flexibility, networking, creativity – that are now key outcomes for students, then the challenge of schooling in the next millennium will not be met.
>
> (1999: 123)

There are difficulties of definition, and many of these stem from over-use of the term 'creativity'. I hope in this chapter to tease out some of the significant characteristics and implications of creativity in the teaching and learning of English, but we need to start from a clear vision. In this respect, the much neglected and, hitherto at least, officially overlooked report of the National Advisory Committee on Creative and Cultural Education, aptly titled *All Our Futures* (NACCCE 1999: 29–30), is helpful. In this report, creativity is defined and presented as 'imaginative activity fashioned so as to produce outcomes that are both original and of value'. This definition is then qualified and elaborated on with reference to four features of creativity: using imagination, pursuing purposes, being original and judging value.

All four features, it seems to me, are vitally important, and the combination provides us with a useful starting point. Clearly, the use of the imagination for a particular purpose is at the heart of the matter – indeed, possibly, at the heart of whatever education is all about. Warnock, for example, holds that the imagination is essentially

> a sense . . . that there is always *more* to experience, and *more in* what we experience than we can predict. Without some such sense, even at the quite human level of there being something which deeply absorbs our interest, human life becomes not actually futile or pointless, but experienced as if it were. It becomes, that is to say, boring. . . . it is the main purpose of education to give people the opportunity of not ever being, in this sense, bored; of not ever succumbing to a sense of futility, or to the belief that they have come to an end of what is worth having.
>
> (Warnock 1976: 202–203)

In this centrally Romantic context, the judgement of value, too, is an easily neglected but crucially significant element, and it is closely linked to the sense of the imagination evoked by Warnock. I would argue that imagination is the means of finding value and, as such, is implicit in all educative processes; its particular significance for English is in the study of the ways in which value and values are embedded in language itself.

Relevant, too, is the idea of originality, although care is needed here to avoid any celebration of originality simply for its own sake, or any inevitably frustrated insistence on total originality – which clearly would be well nigh impossible to achieve except at some cutting edge activity in any given discipline. In a way, of course, everything is original, in that the precise circumstances and conditions are unique to the occurrence; in another way, nothing is – for we must always work with whatever resources and ideas already exist. The English classroom should acknowledge both these apparently contradictory senses of originality – celebrating the moments of creativity on the one hand, and working within the discipline of study on the other. The emphasis in the context of *All Our Futures* is on individual originality ('a person's work may be original in relation to their own previous work and output') or on relative originality ('original in relation to their peer group; to other young people of the same age, for example'), and it would not be hard to find excellent examples of both in our schools – although actual recognition of what we find might be rather more of a challenge, and perhaps would be more unusual.

In classroom practice, it is the dynamic relationship between the previously cited four elements (using imagination, pursuing purposes, being original, judging value), and the skills needed to realise them, that gives rise to meaningful creativity. And yet the subject English itself is not always seen or constructed primarily as a 'creative' discipline – indeed, the current emphasis on functional literacy may be seen as something of an erosion of notions of creativity in the classroom. As Marshall (in Craft *et al.* 2001: 123) points out, the *All Our Futures* report makes scant reference to English, being

> a good example of the way in which English is no longer considered central to the arts debate. In the appendix, which considers the impact of their proposals, English does not appear anywhere within the list of arts subjects. The contribution of English acknowledged in the body of the document is equally marginal.

Part of our intention in this book is to re-place English as an arts subject, with all that entails and implies, making full use of the insights into creativity in such texts as *All Our Futures*. It should also be clear by now that literacy itself, if construed in broad terms of meaning, value and an intercultural context, as well as function, need not necessarily be narrow in scope.

Creativity, if it is to mean anything significant in practice, certainly needs a place from which it may thrive. As ever, the language we use in this context is highly suggestive. The noun 'place' implies a fixed site: there seems to be something definite, permanent, even immovable about the term. Where precisely this place may be is another matter: could it be the physical base of the classroom? Or the school itself? Or, more abstractly, might it be found in the curriculum, or in the particularities of the various subjects which make up that curriculum, or especially in the discipline of English studies? All of these are interesting, even provocative, possibilities. However, as the form of the English language requires, it is the accompanying verb that qualifies, amplifies and clarifies the noun, thus making fuller exploratory sense of the issues. Here, it is possible to speak of discovering, recognising, exploring and celebrating the place – indeed, I would argue that each of these active approaches has, in its turn, a vital place in the development of creativity. After all, a place remains just a place without the verb denoting human social action to make – create, in effect – sense and meaning out of its latent possibilities. Our approaches to 'place' as teachers and learners need not be limited, clearly, by the four verbs suggested above. Nevertheless, they seem to me vital in realising the creative potential of the educational places we find ourselves in – in both abstract and concrete terms – and will inform subsequent exploration during this chapter and beyond. To pursue the linguistic connotations just a little further, it is interesting to explore the word 'place' as, itself, a verb. If, indeed, we find, as teachers, that creativity is not in place, despite our attempts to discover, recognise, explore and celebrate, then it is up to us as active participants to 'place' (or perhaps 're-place'?) it there. By envisaging the word as an active force in itself, its radically participative and trans-formational possibilities may be released: teachers and learners creating and developing the appropriate conditions for ourselves.

Creativity as placed, or as place, is not without its tensions and diffi-culties. At the time of writing there are widespread concerns that, whatever it is, creativity needs more careful nurturing in our schools – that, in one way or another, it is somehow under threat. To cite just two examples: the *Times Educational Supplement* ran a highly prominent series during the first half of 2003 aimed at safeguarding and protecting creativity in schools, and the Qualifications and Curriculum Authority (QCA) has launched (Summer 2003) a wide-ranging 'National Curriculum in Action' initiative, apparently with the enthusiastic blessing of the Secretary of State, Charles Clarke, under the slogan 'Creativity: Find It, Promote It' (see www. ncaction.org.uk). We have seen already, in Chapter 1, how important it is for the English teacher to 'find it', with reference to the pupil's piece of writing 'Kyle's Split Knee': sometimes creativity can be discovered, if not differentiated, by outcome rather than explicit intention. In this context, readiness is all. The QCA initiative may be seen, perhaps cynically, as a belated and rather embarrassed response to the *All Our Futures* publica-tion of four years previously – but at least it shows an acknowledgement of the key issues. All this rather begs some important questions concerning the meaning and validity of creativity, and why it is especially valuable. If, indeed, it is valuable, then a sense of value lies at its heart. As has been suggested previously, in discussions about instrumental rationality and its implications, it is possible to act creatively, as is commonly understood by the term, for highly questionable ends: exploitative, destructive, damaging. To make radical social meaning in the context of teaching and learning, creativity needs to be situated in a coherent place of values. Creativity's minute particularities, its celebratory subjectivities, its potential for social meaning-making, its liberating connective power only really come to life when values are emphasised.

But what and whose values? As so often, the answer lies in the framing of the question: in the sense that values are culturally specific and, as such, are contested – often energetically, sometimes creatively, and sometimes destructively. There are, indeed, multiple places for creativity, and each relates to the cultural context. In a way, this implies multiculturalism, but

I am, here, more interested in the connections between places, and by this route between creativity and value. With the stress on connections – relationships, contrasts, compatibilities – it may be more helpful to suggest an intercultural rather than merely a multicultural understanding of creativity and value. The implication of this kind of understanding is that creativity may be placed in multiple sites and have roots in diverse cultural values, and that it is in the relationships between these entities – the 'inter' of the intercultural project – that deep value-laden meaning may be both found and made. Importantly, this conception is suggestive of both individual and social transformation, as the damaging distinction between the two is eroded. As Alred *et al.* (2003: 4–5) have clarified:

> The locus of interaction is not in the centripetal reinforcement of the identity of one group and its members by contrast with others, but rather in the centrifugal action of each which creates a new centre of interaction on the borders and frontiers which join rather than divide them. This centre is experienced not only in relation to others, but also in relation to oneself. ... An inevitable consequence of intercultural experience is that it presents a challenge to customary modes of perception, thought and feeling. Hence, when intercultural experience leads to creative, rather than defensive, learning a concomitant is serious self-reflection and examination, bringing with it consequences for self-understanding and self-knowledge. ... Frontiers become less barriers and prohibitions and more gateways and invitations.

Interestingly, Holbrook, as cited by McGuinn in Chapter 3, uses the same metaphor of the 'gateway' for a different, if similarly liberating, purpose. This is a highly significant perception, and the implications for the intercultural English classroom – the irony of this formulation is interesting in itself – will be explored more fully by McGuinn in Chapter 3 and by me in Chapter 6. Relevant here, especially, is Alred's distinction between creative rather than defensive responses – which leads us back to the contextual exploration of creativity in English teaching.

At this juncture it may be helpful to consider the possible structure of the classroom-based experience we may wish to foster. At the heart of the creative project there must be cognisance of difference and diversity: 'One law for the lion and the ox is oppression', as we have heard Blake defiantly proclaim. Or, in rather more prosaic terms: 'creativity is a basic capacity of human intelligence. Human intelligence is not only creative, but multi-faceted. ... all young people have creative capacities and they all have them differently' (NACCCE 1999: 34).

The problem is that uniformity in schooling tends to ignore these differences in favour of a model of education that remains predominantly industrial by nature: regimented, teacher focused, didactic, governed by 'clocking in' procedures, specific lengths of time, and, of course, by the school bell. There is considerable potential for ICT, in its more liberating manifestations and implications, to challenge this kind of regimentation – a theme McGuinn returns to in Chapter 5. The answer is assuredly not to be found in some sort of erosion of the comprehensive principle in favour of one subject specialism or another, or some other sort of special status, which is ultimately likely to replicate the characteristics of conformity in a context of inequality, and without the emphasis on equality of opportunity that is, or certainly should be, deeply embedded in the comprehensive principle.

At the centre of concern here is what Brecht aptly called 'Lebenskunst', the creative art of life itself. If intercultural variety and vitality are the aims, they must also be the means – and the culture of the classroom is that which both stimulates and emanates from the totality of experience. That familiar unit of school-based time, the lesson – with all its generally ignored spiritual connotations fully acknowledged here – must, in some sense or other, become a microcosm of broader issues. I have in mind here, particularly, a Romantic transformative model, through which innocence is brought into some sort of relationship – even one based on conflict – with experience. In a fully dialectical process, fostered by careful teaching, the interplay between innocence as thesis and experience as antithesis may lead to a higher, fuller awareness – based on innocence in the Blakean sense of wonder, but acknowledging and encompassing the nature of, often harsh, experience. This culmination may be conceptualised as a kind of synthesis which, of course, will then play its part in further dialectical encounters. For the Romantics – Blake perhaps especially – this sort of transformative model provided insights into the development of the human psyche, individually, historically and socially. In the same way as each individual struggles in his or her life with this fundamental transformative process in a fully social context, so too must human institutions and the various elements that comprise them. School itself is one of the most basic of those institutions, but I am more interested here in smaller, more manageable units within school: the lesson, particularly, and the classroom. Interestingly too, the age range of the schools we are dealing with here (roughly 11–18) precisely includes the time when the clash (or, sometimes, harmony) between innocence and experience is most striking. (The story written by the Malaysian pupil, Nasrullah, cited by McGuinn in Chapter 3, is a particularly striking example of this tension.) Any concern for a truly creative classroom culture must start from this realisation; conversely, failure fully to acknowledge the inter-relationship leads all too often to endless unresolved conflicts in schools. As Nobel (1996: 37) observes: 'It is a matter of seeking out ways of reaching a development of knowledge which looks to *the whole person*, which in itself is a prerequisite for the person himself [*sic*] being able to see the *whole comprehensive context*.'

So if each lesson, as a microcosm of the wider context, may be conceptualised along these fundamentally Romantic lines, the results may lead to
some interesting speculations. The basic point is that a lesson or a lesson
plan is a culturally loaded text like anything else and, as such, should
certainly be subject to critical evaluation. As we expect learning to unfold
so, as teachers, we conceive of, shape and construct our lessons. I looked
at possible lesson structures in Chapter 1, with particular reference to aims
and objectives, and the three-stage format suggested there fits neatly, and
creatively, into the Romantic model. This structure is not intended as rigid
or restrictive but, rather, as offering suggestive guidelines. The opening
phase in the structure is essentially an exploratory stage, broadly characterised by innocence – attempting to see the theme or subject as if new,
without prejudice, in a way open to intercultural interplay of viewpoints.
The middle phase would be more akin to the onset and management of
experience, through which ideas, meanings and interpretations are tested
against the rigours of worldly experience – including, crucially, the experiences of the students themselves. As for Blake, experience reminds us that
all is not necessarily easy and well in the world, even if the classroom may
afford some shelter from exploitative excesses and lead to a false sense of
well being:

> It is an easy thing to triumph in the summer's sun
> And in the vintage, and to sing on the wagon loaded with corn.
> It is an easy thing to talk of patience to the afflicted . . .
> To hear the dog howl at the wintry door, the ox in the
>   slaughterhouse moan;
> To see a god on every wind and a blessing on every blast . . .
> It is an easy thing to rejoice in the tents of prosperity:
> Thus could I sing and thus rejoice: but it is not so with me.
>
>   (Blake, from *Vala or the Four Zoas*)

This kind of reminder, focusing on the juxtaposition of easy luxury and
acute hardship in our society and eliciting sensitive, apt responses, has
always been part of the English curriculum. In the best English classrooms,
through literary, linguistic or thematic exploration, serious issues are
confronted – and it should be especially so in the intercultural context
proposed here. The final stage within the lesson structure, what I described
previously as the 'making, sharing and critical evaluation of artefacts',
would be an attempt at creative, perhaps celebratory, synthesis. A valid
plenary should draw things together meaningfully, while simultaneously
suggesting an openness to new ideas and interpretations for subsequent

exploration. In such a model as this, teachers may best be envisaged as 'transformative practitioners', skilfully managing the often disparate but always connected elements involved. English lessons may, indeed, become *Songs of Innocence and of Experience*.

As W. B. Yeats observed, 'education should be not filling a bucket but lighting a fire'. Structures, however imaginatively conceived, tend to become ends in themselves – further examples of instrumental rationality, mere buckets to be filled – unless the creative fire is stimulated. The signs of creativity are indeed varied, often hard to discern, but are there to discover or make nevertheless. Bill Lucas has offered a helpful list of some of the characteristics of what he terms, appropriately enough, learner-centred creativity (Lucas 2001: 40). These are:

- Being respectful rather than dismissive
- Encouraging active not passive learning
- Supporting individual interests rather than standardised curriculums
- Engaging many learning styles not one
- Encouraging and exploring emotional responses
- Posing questions not statements
- Offering ambiguities rather than certainties
- Being open-ended rather than closing down
- Being surprising rather than predictable
- Offering many patterns rather than a standardised model
- Moving the 'classroom' to varied environments
- Recognising multiple intelligences
- Including visual representations as well as auditory ones
- Including tactile and experience-based activity
- Stimulating social as well as private learning.

In many ways the recognition of some or all of these qualities helps us as teachers to define something that can sometimes seem very nebulous, as long as definitions are regarded as tentative openings rather than as restrictive impositions. In this sense, it is important that both teachers and learners experience a sense of involvement in, and ownership of, the creativity in the classroom through what Gardner has called 'good work'. Anything else would clearly run counter to the very nature of creativity in education. The Chicago psychologist Csikszentmihalyi (1990) has conceptualised creativity as the experience of 'flow' or 'optimal experience', suggestive of engagement, empathy, connection, interplay; such a formulation sits easily with the intercultural model proposed here. Further characteristic symptoms, according to the 'flow' model, would include complete involvement in the activity through both intellect and feeling, immediate feedback through an intrinsic sense of the worth of the activity in and for itself, and an appropriate balance of challenge and capability. In respect of all this, it seems to me essential that the subject English – and, by implication, its teaching – is conceived of in terms of an artistic endeavour, in the sense that Iris Murdoch meant: 'Art is not a diversion or a side issue. It is the most educational of human activities and a place in which the nature of morality can be seen' (in NACCCE 1999: 67). The fundamental question, of course, is whether any or all of these qualities can be recognised in the English classroom. In instances of good practice – good work, in effect – many, indeed, can be; it seems to me that the potential, however, is for a great deal more.

So, at the risk of appearing to seek an exhaustive definition for something that by its very nature must constantly strive to burst boundaries, it is important that creativity is positively recognised in the classroom. In many ways it is the opposite that is more obvious. As Boden (in Craft *et al.* 2001: 98) points out:

> It is easy enough to say what will smother creativity in the classroom: three things above all. First, an unbending insistence on the 'right' answer, and/or on the 'right' way of finding it; second, an unwillingness (or inability) to analyse the 'wrong' answer to see whether it might have some merit, perhaps in somewhat different circumstances ... ; and third, an expression of impatience, or (worse still) contempt, for the person who came up with the unexpected answer.

Although there is a clear distinction to be made between teaching creatively, which may cover a vast range of pedagogical models, and teaching for creativity, the two frequently complement each other. Ultimately my emphasis here is on teaching for creativity, but the role of the teacher as creative practitioner – modelling the qualities sought in the learner – is fundamental. Characteristics of good teaching practice in this respect – teaching creatively to foster creativity – are necessarily diverse: the giving of early and meaningful opportunities for all to excel in some aspect of the work covered; the successful communication that risk-taking is acceptable even when unsuccessful; the teaching of the skills necessary in any particular discipline for satisfaction to be realisable; the stimulation of a supportive, critical-friendly classroom culture; and the tolerance of difference. Language and meaning – literacy in its broadest sense – are crucial in the actualisation of all or any of these qualities, which is one good reason why they should be central to English teaching.

Safran (in Craft *et al.* 2001: 82) appropriately terms teaching for purposes such as those outlined here 'mindful teaching', suggesting further that, consequently, 'mindful learning' should form its complement:

In defining 'to teach' I draw on its original meaning 'to show'. . . . Mindful teaching facilitates learning by showing, explaining or passing on a skill or knowledge while being mindful of the subject matter, open to new information, creating new categories and being aware of many perspectives within the subject matter. More importantly, the mindful teacher is also mindful of the learner, that is open to their perspectives, and receptive to information from the learner. The mindful teacher is therefore learner-led. A mindful teacher begins from where the learner is and opens up the unknown, showing new possibilities to the learner at a pace appropriate to them. . . . The mindful teacher makes critical thought possible for the learner through questioning the learner, showing them areas and avenues the learner may not yet have discovered for themselves.

What is beginning to emerge from all this, hopefully (in both grammatical senses), is the sense that teaching for creativity is quite a tall order, requiring the courage of conviction, yet is within the pedagogical potential of the classroom teacher. In effect, this means that an appropriate balance between challenge and capability should be sought and modelled through teaching, as noted above in the context purely of learning.

Tentatively summarising and developing the various suggestions already made, it may be helpful to pause here to recollect and specify some of the characteristics of what could be called a creative classroom. Above all there must be concern for the meaningful generation and practical implementation of ideas and feelings, even when unexpected and unplanned, through the making of varied and sometimes unusual connections and contrasts. Planning is, thus, to be seen as a process rather than a fixed or rigid imposition on the flow of a lesson, achieved ultimately through the conscious, reflective refinement and development of one's own (or the group's own) activities. Inevitably, any creative act, and certainly any creative lesson, involves the teacher in the release and appropriate channelling of energy. The creative teacher seeks ways of inventing, adapting, extending and completing tasks in new or exciting ways – completion being particularly important in response to the charge, frequently levelled in my experience, and with some justification, that anyone can be creative for short snatches without being able necessarily to sustain any real momentum towards fruition. Alertness is vital, in both senses of the word, seeking and seeing possibilities for the use of diverse resources, and always remembering that the best resources, linguistic or otherwise, are the people in the classroom. Ultimately there has to be a sense of value in teaching and learning: it is not too grandiose an ambition to seek to change the world for the better, enhancing the *quality* of life – especially in the active embodiment of aesthetic and celebratory dimensions. The imagination is fundamental in this context for both teacher and learners, in the sense that, as Blake had it, 'what is now proved was once only imagined'. Throughout all this and much more, for even these tentative suggestions can do no real justice to a vividly creative classroom, there has to be a genuinely reflective awareness of the possibilities for continual re-interpretation and re-formulation of materials, 'knowledge' and meaning.

Throughout all these areas, as has been previously suggested, one formulation remains absolutely central; it is, in the words of Herbert Read, that 'art, widely conceived, should be the fundamental basis of education'. The word 'art' itself connotes a great deal more than is often, rather narrowly, supposed; Hagerstrand makes the interesting point that

> in both research and practice it is necessary to revive the original double meaning of the concept 'art' which previously encompassed both practical skill and works of 'fine culture'. It ought to present itself as a fascinating task to so permeate, by means of research and teaching, the personal philosophy of people with a new aesthetic keynote that their philosophy would become strong enough to keep narrow rationality, fanaticism and commercial tricks at bay. . . . That thought is an interesting challenge to all those engaged in the business of teaching.
>
> (in Nobel, 1996: 25)

It is indeed, and this book is, in part, an attempt to take up the challenge, as indicated in the title itself, suggestive of both of Hagerstrand's meanings. In this sense, teaching is itself an art, and also part of the bigger – and aesthetically stimulating – intercultural landscape.

I return next to Blake, here less in terms of a guiding spirit behind the ideas in this book, and more as a writer to be taught – although the two are sometimes impossible to separate. Much of what follows is based on research I undertook on the teaching of Blake's *Songs of Innocence and of Experience* to a group of fourteen Year 12 (16–17 year old) students specialising in English literature. I was particularly focusing on notions of what types of literal and non-literal understanding may be achieved through study of Blake's writing, and how the poems might connect to the students' broader cultural experiences, in the sense that, as Rogoff observes,

> an individual's actions and skills cannot be understood out of the context of the immediate practical goals being sought and the enveloping socio-cultural goals into which they fit. It is the communities to which they belong that provide the communicative tools for organising and understanding experience and generating new knowledge.
>
> (Rogoff 1999, cited by Leach in
> Craft *et al.* 2001: 180)

The immediate teaching context was to spend a term on Blake, based on a weekly session of one hour and forty minutes, culminating in a written coursework assignment focusing on an understanding of the relationship between innocence and experience in his writing. Early in Year 12 as it was, in their second term of study, the students had little experience of close textual reading, and none of Blake. In a sense, they were 'innocent' of the sophisticated wiles of A Level literary study. Following the Blakean three-part lesson outlined previously, our initial phase was innocent enough, 'playing' with a range of resources focused on Blake: some of the poems from *Songs of Innocence and of Experience*; on separate sheets, Blake's accompanying illustrations; some of his other paintings and prints; a few of Blake's more provocative aphorisms from *The Marriage of Heaven and Hell* and elsewhere; and other artefacts touching on Blake (including Van Morrison's *If the Slave* . . . and John Tavener's versions of *The Tiger* and *The Lamb* on CD, and a video of Alan Ginsberg singing *The Tiger* to a harmonium accompaniment). The diversity of art-forms – text, music and pictorial arts – not only fitted Blake's own talents and interests, but, peda-gogically, fitted appropriately into this 'innocent', playful phase. Again, and not only because the subject was Blake, the idea is profoundly Romantic – in the sense that the Romantic poet and philosopher Friedrich Schiller indi-cated when he wrote that 'Man plays only when he is, in the full meaning of the word, Man, and is only wholly Man when at play' (from 'On the Aesthetic Education of Man'). Nobel (1996: 100) has helpfully elaborated on the importance of 'play' from Schiller's perspective, as 'analogous to art. In his play man [*sic*] is free to put real objects from the outside world into contexts which give him satisfaction. . . . In this way the person play-ing stamps his subjectivity onto reality and gives subjectivity in turn objective validity'.

McGuinn explores the nature of play as a centrally Romantic notion more fully in Chapter 4. My intention for this lesson was simply to stimu-late work in groups of three to collect and subsequently re-present a selection of the available resources according to taste, without attempting to analyse too deeply. The results were startling in the enterprise shown by the students in using the images and each other to spark off ideas and perceptions, and the activity certainly served its purpose in whetting the appetite – mine as well as theirs – for more of Blake.

The next phase, introducing an element of socio-historical contextual-ising experience into the frame, took the form of my brief exposition of Blake's life and times, aided by clips from a couple of videos of BBC programmes on Blake. If achieving nothing else, this session served to remind me of the sixth-form students' general lack of awareness and know-ledge of the historical and cultural context Blake worked in. I was acutely conscious that, without a grounding of contextual insight, it would be unlikely that there could be any kind of deeper creative response to or understanding of the verse, for, as Boden (in Craft *et al.* 2001: 102) puts it: 'Creativity is not the same thing as knowledge, but is firmly grounded in it. What educators must try to do is to nurture the knowledge without killing the creativity.' This is an intercultural concern as well as a literary-contextual one, in the very basic sense that we're really speaking about building bridges between cultural vantage points past and present. I attempted to make this session as interactive as possible by asking students, working in pairs, to jot down responses to such terms as 'romantic', 'imagination', 'innocence' and 'experience', and to historically relevant details like '1789', 'the French Revolution', 'the slave trade' and 'the American War of Independence'. Certain interesting ideas did emerge, which gave us useful starting points – linking 'imagination' with 'innocence', for example – but there were few accurate perceptions of the broadly historical phenomena. In the end I talked through some of the relevant areas from the *Resource Notes* of my edition of Blake, which we were using, including the time line, and recommended a more thorough individual study before our next session.

The following week, the group, working in different pairs, went on to study self-selected poems – one each from *Innocence* and *Experience* – in the light of questions focusing on what may be understood literally and what metaphorically from a first reading, and how the two relate to each other. The basic questions I posed in an attempt to elicit this distinction were:

1   In your chosen poems, list the main images; what is your understanding of them in terms of their literal reality in your experience?
2   Explore possible connotations of these images, in terms of your own ideas and Blake's use of them in the poems. Do they 'work' for you as pictures in your mind's eye?

As a whole group we discussed these and related questions briefly, as the distinction between literal and metaphorical is an elusive one, before moving on to the task itself. I deliberately chose the pairs, attempting to combine students whose approaches and sympathies I thought would contrast, even conflict. Indeed, monitoring these explorations, I became conscious of a split developing within the group between those receptive – often quite excitedly – to Blake's ideas on the power of the imagination, and those who, not to put too fine a point on it, were becoming bored. Attraction or otherwise to Blake seemed to depend on attitudes towards conventionality in terms of thought and behaviour. Several of the group aspired to more unconventional ways of thinking, and they tended to find Blake a sympathetic figure at least in terms of the ideas expressed in the poems we studied: the liberating quality of the imagination and, by the same token, the limited nature of 'normal' consciousness. Others in the group took what may be described as a more common-sense approach, tending to dismiss Blake as 'weird' – in similar terms to those used by his contemporary detractors. Clearly, an appreciation of literature and its possible personal impact depends largely on attitudes already formed: imaginary experience depends on the thoughts, feelings and relationships readers can actively bring to bear from their own personal lives. Take, for example, this extracted exchange on *The Clod and the Pebble*:

Student A:	It's about a clod of clay being squashed . . . but why write a poem about it?
Student B:	And what about the pebble . . . surely a pebble can't float . . .
Student A:	Perhaps it doesn't really matter . . . maybe it's really about two different types of people . . . one's a clod who gets stamped on . . . maybe he's too kind and generous and then gets walked over . . .
Student B:	Squelch of mud oozing everywhere . . . it still seems silly to me: a poem about mud . . .

And so the conversation continued. One train of thought led from the poem to expand its possible implications and meanings, while returning constantly for fresh insights. The other got bogged down – if the expression may be forgiven in this context – in the idea that meaningful, sensitive poetry just cannot be written about lumps of earth and small pebbles. Similar conversations took place on other poems, and in the subsequent whole-group discussions. As both teacher and researcher, I was anxious not to give interpretations of the poems, but to allow students to grapple with the possibilities and complexities at this stage with little explicit guidance.

Emerging here are crucial questions concerning who reads Blake's work and how it may be interpreted. The impossibility, and undesirability, of a definitive reading of any text has to be continually underlined by the nature of our teaching approaches and activities, and this was certainly my aim in teaching, publishing and researching Blake. I can think of no better author to illustrate this sense of the reader's interpretive power over the text: his openness to the possibilities of multiple readings and levels of understanding is a significant part of that robustness to which I alluded earlier. However, this does leave an important role for the teacher, in the sense that guidance may well be required before deeper, more satisfying readings can be achieved. I was also acutely conscious of needing to dispel the all too prevalent 'hidden meanings' conception of poetry, whereby the text is seen as some sort of coded puzzle needing only a particular key to uncover the 'real' meaning. Some of the difficulties experienced by several of the group

– and other students I have encountered subsequently – stemmed, I think, from the non-literal nature of Blake's verse. For the literal-minded, indeed, the work can appear strange: the *Songs of Innocence* may come across as mere nursery rhymes about lambs and angels – which, in one sense, they are: Blake himself delighted in children's enthusiasm for the songs. The point is to foster a genuine, full engagement with the experience of learning, as Nobel (1996: 104) maintains:

> The student as well as teacher must be in a position of continuously experiencing as well as creating the knowledge and the material with which he [*sic*] comes into contact. Without such an inner effort, and the formative, shaping aspects which it involves, no real insight is achieved.

In this sense, a literal reading is likely to be limited and partial rather than faulty, lacking the potential to develop beyond a rather one-dimensional appraisal. For another of the *Experience* songs, *The Sick Rose*, the following brief extract from a discussion between four of the students, combining two of the pairs who had chosen the same poem, is indicative of the contrasting approaches:

Student A:	What I can't see is: how does a worm fly? I mean I've never seen a flying worm, have you?
Student B:	Maybe it's a special sort of worm . . .
Student A:	(sarcastically) Yeah, it could be extinct by now . . .
Student C:	But it doesn't make any difference: the worm's an evil force, isn't it? It's symbolic.
Student D:	(resignedly) Oh, that again . . .

A familiar tangle? One of the difficulties here for the teacher is in avoiding a hierarchical view of different interpretations, with the symbolic lauding it over rather more literal receptions of the poetry: this would clearly militate against the openness of interpretive approach which underlies imaginative literature teaching. In a sense, however, we are not talking here of a particular interpretation being correct, or better than another but, rather, about *modes* of interpretation. If literature is to be explored and fruitful connections made with other experiences of life – other cultures in effect – we need to equip our students with the appropriate interpretive tools. What is especially interesting about the sort of exchange quoted briefly above is that the literal interpretation, glib as it is, does not actually lead anywhere: it is unable to transcend its own literalness. Paradoxically, the less literal the approach, the more vivid is the image: witness Student C's 'evil force' idea. Effective English teaching elicits and develops such responses, but the very openness of discussion begs the question: what is the role of the teacher here? In the end, surely, the role of the teacher must be to teach, and fundamental to that is the making available to students some of the possible modes of textual, intertextual and contextual under-standing. Over-arching all of this, clearly, is the intercultural dimension – for all texts and contexts derive from, illustrate and creatively lead away from intercultural cross-fertilisation.

My term's work on Blake continued through a more detailed appraisal of Blake's poems, increasingly focusing on definitions of, and the relation-ship between, innocence and experience. What emerged, excitingly for me, was a gathering appreciation of the link between Blake's concept of innocence and the non-literal understanding of the world, and, corre-spondingly, the close resemblance of Blake's experience to literalness. As Blake's terms suggest, our primary understanding may well be of the non-literal type, later to be replaced by experienced literal approaches. One student, studying language acquisition as part of her English Language A Level course, was able to bring her research in this area to bear on the question, relating how her investigations suggested that young children attach imaginative, symbolic meanings to words, culled from a wide range of contexts including songs and stories. We worked through several of the activities featured in the *Cambridge* Blake, including collage work, dramatic approaches such as hot-seating and scripted meetings between characters from different poems (the various lost children of *Innocence* and *Experience*, for example), and musical associations and interpretations. Inevitably, though, lack of time in an overcrowded syllabus precluded more exhaustive study. The students also kept a detailed log of their study of Blake, highlighting four poems from *Innocence* and four from *Experience* which would provide the basis of their subsequent written assignments. In my view we achieved a measure of synthesis between the contrasting approaches, without some of the group ever quite abandoning their literal readings. Not that this was the aim, for all the limited scope of such read-ings and, again, Blake's robustness allows even for dismissive responses. The period of study culminated in an essay on the relationship between innocence and experience in Blake's work, couched in deliberately open-ended terms to allow for a range of responses drawing on previous discussions and readings. The resulting writing varied along the lines of our many debates. One of the group wrote by way of conclusion:

> There is always something particularly alluring in a figure with an immense talent which he chooses to use in a radical way. A feeling of sympathy usually arises for such a character, especially in a situation where you feel

the person is practically burdened by the sheer weight of their ability . . .
The arts world is littered with such people – they are said to be 'burned
out' but these are the ones that will be always remembered. There is a
saying 'shooting stars shine the brightest'.

The essay itself, as may be witnessed even in the brief extract quoted
here, was characterised by a genuinely fruitful discussion: interweaving
with the text of the poems but never a slave to it, achieving a vivid sense
of textual engagement through elaborating on rather than simply analysing
the art itself. I feel that examples of students' writing such as this – and all
English teachers will have met them – may be seen as typifying the third
stage of the Romantic lesson plan: a creative synthesis of innocent and
experienced approaches, leaving scope to discover and invent more. As
such, it is a fitting tribute to the power of creativity.

In Blake we have an important ally in this project, not only in providing
texts to study, but, rather more profoundly, in offering an insight into the
nature of intercultural education through his art. The preposition *through*
is significant here: as we have already noted, Blake himself calls for seeing
as understanding as opposed to merely recognising, for

> We are led to believe a lie
> when we see not through the eye
> (from *Auguries of Innocence*)

Critical engagement and felt empathy are fundamental parts of this kind
of understanding – an essentially questioning approach. But there is also
scope for intuition, for seeing the whole entity through giving the faculty
of insight a chance to operate. In this sense, Blake would surely have agreed
with Wittgenstein that 'People who are constantly asking "why" are like
tourists who stand in front of a building reading Baedecker and are so busy
reading the history of its construction, etc., that they are prevented from
seeing the building' (1940; in Guilherme 2002: 117).

Part of any creative response to the world and word and, indeed, part
of any proposed resolution of tensions, must centrally involve intuition and
what is increasingly acknowledged as 'emotional literacy'. In terms of the
arguments presented here, I agree entirely with Guilherme (2002: 37) when
she maintains that:

> Being a critical thinker involves more than being rational and emotion
> is not viewed as an inferior cognitive stage. Emotion is given a key role
> in CP [Critical Pedagogy] in that it is considered as a fundamental stim-
> ulus for cognitive, interpretive, critical and creative reflection-in-action.

The following examples may serve to illustrate and even illuminate this aspect of teaching and learning.

A good deal of the creative enjoyment inherent in English teaching lies in the selection of, and the making of connections between, appropriate texts. If anything, in an increasingly crowded curriculum, there is now a greater need than ever to exercise this skill, and to ensure that as many as possible learning outcomes – to use the officially favoured term – are covered in the process of their teaching. I have used these texts and extracts in a range of classroom contexts, across a 14–18 age range, sometimes individually and at other times in various combinations. They are:

- 'Reading Pictures' – three expanding versions of a photograph of a soldier apparently aiming his rifle out of the window of a derelict house, strewn with debris including a headless doll (published by the British Film Institute).
- The lyrics and recorded version of a Richard Thompson song *How will I ever be simple again?* from his 1986 Polydor album *Daring Adventures*.
- The Henry Treece poem *Conquerors*, which centres on the accumulating guilt and grief of an invading soldier through the succeeding images of a dead bird in an abandoned cage, a starving homeless dog, and, finally, a dead child. The poem includes the memorable lines:

  > Not one amongst us would have eaten bread
  > Before he'd filled the mouth of the grey child
  > That sprawled, stiff as stone, before the shattered door.

- A printed and audio-recorded extract from the opening stages of Fergal Keane's autobiographical *Letter to Daniel*.

The unifying theme of the texts is to do with the relationship between innocence and experience, thus modelling a favourite Romantic preoccupation – the innocence represented by facets of childhood, directly or indirectly; and war providing the backdrop, human experience at its most brutal and destructive. There is an interesting range of possible further poems appropriate to this theme, several of which have been anthologised in the collection *Peace and War*, chosen by Harrison and Stuart-Clark (1989). They include W. H. Auden's *Epitaph on a Tyrant*, Stephen Crane's ironic *War is Kind*, Denise Levertov's reflections on Vietnam *What Were They Like?*, Alun Lewis's *All Day it has Rained*, Dennis McHarrie's *Luck*, Wilfred Owen's *Futility* (among several others), Siegfried Sassoon's *Suicide in the Trenches*, William Soutar's *The Children*, and Dylan Thomas's elegiac *A Refusal to Mourn the Death, by Fire, of a Child in London*. The stark contrast between a sense of wonder on the one hand and Owen's 'pity of war' on the other provides a moving tension at the heart of this learning, and of course there are many other texts which could also be tellingly deployed here.

There is clearly a danger that study of such texts as these could give rise to the idea that war, destruction and violence happen only in far off places or in the distant past, and intercultural teaching must acknowledge this. As so often, the way forward, it seems to me, lies in focusing on the tension between emotional empathy – and it is not hard to see this elicited by these texts – and critical distance. In asking questions about responsibility for the consequences of human actions, such texts and their effective teaching, provide a way back into more immediate social reality. It is important, too, to introduce variety of textual form, if only to show that it is not just the poet who feels the pity. Here, for instance, there are pictures, autobiographical prose, the human voice speaking and singing, a song, and a poem – and each extends possible areas of intertextual literacy. Teaching like this has also to be sensitive to the possible responses of pupils, especially if at the younger end of the age range, to the harrowing scenes evoked – that is part of the fine judgement English teachers, particularly, have often to make.

The possibilities for imaginative teaching arising from these texts, and others like them, are vast in scope. All of the suggestions below have been effective in stimulating critical and creative learning activity; the main point is, however, that confident teachers can adapt and adopt freely from these and their own chosen resources. Often, if the initial enthusiasm is there, the appropriate learning outcomes will follow; or, as Blake had it in his *Proverbs of Hell*, 'No bird soars too high, if he soars on his own wings'. Some activities:

- learning focused on intertextual empathy, experimenting with characters and viewpoints across the texts;
- narrative exploration – using the 'moment' of the text as narrative starting point, or linking the different texts together in a broader narrative;
- a study of war reportage, and specifically how the language used – its inevitable characteristics and conventions – is dialectically and critically linked to meaning;
- thematic work on 'war and peace', using the texts among others as the basis of descriptive or persuasive presentations, articles, displays or collages;
- discursive explorations of the nature of innocence and experience – not necessarily just as characteristic of children and adults, but as Blake's 'two contrary states of the human soul'.

In order to give a fuller flavour of the resources and activities outlined, I include a substantial extract from Fergal Keane's *Letter to Daniel: Despatches from the Heart*:

Hong Kong, February 1996

Daniel Patrick Keane was born on 4 February 1996.

. . . In a world of insecurity and ambition and ego, it's easy to be drawn in, to take chances with our lives, to believe that what we do and what people say about us is reason enough to gamble with death. Now, looking at your sleeping face, inches away from me, listening to your occasional sigh and gurgle, I wonder how I could have ever thought glory and prizes and praise were sweeter than life.

And it's also true that I am pained, perhaps haunted is a better word, by the memory, suddenly so vivid now, of each suffering child I have come across on my journeys. To tell you the truth, it's nearly too much to bear at this moment to even think of children being hurt and abused and killed. And yet looking at you, the images come flooding back.

. . . There is one last memory. Of Rwanda, and the churchyard of the parish of Nyarabuye where, in a ransacked classroom, I found a mother and her three young children huddled together where they'd been beaten to death. The children had died holding on to their mother, that instinct we all learn from birth and in one way or another cling to until we die.

3   Romantic words and worlds

'Poetry's the speech of kings'. You're one of those
Shakespeare gives the comic bits to: prose.
(Tony Harrison, *Them [and Uz]*)

Is it possible to take a Romantic perspective on twenty-first century literacy teaching? I want to begin my response to the challenges posed by Stevens in Chapters 1 and 2 with a brief story. Not long ago, I was trying to teach Tennyson's poem *Mariana* to a class of fifteen-year-olds in a northern comprehensive school. The pupils were members of a lower-set GCSE English Literature group. I remember one particular boy (I'll call him Alan) who, though clearly intelligent and articulate, made it vociferously clear that he had no desire to engage with the delights of nineteenth-century poetry. Late one Friday afternoon, when we were all tired and waiting for the bell to release us, Alan surprised and exasperated me by taking a momentary break from his quietly sustained disruption to observe that the final word of Tennyson's famous line *The blue fly sung in the pane* was a pun which symbolised the silent, claustrophobic suffering of the poem's heroine. When the lesson was over, I asked him – in the way that teachers do – why, since he was clearly a sensitive and perceptive reader of poetry, he was not prepared to make that kind of contribution all the time. Alan replied that he was just counting the days till he could leave school and take up his uncle's offer of a job on a building-site. The acquisition of an examination certificate in English Literature was of no interest to him at all.

Looking back at that incident, I can see how my response to Alan was shaped by key Romantic principles which, in the mid years of the twentieth century, vitally informed the teaching of English in general and literacy in particular. Why had I chosen to teach such a text – seemingly so unsuitable in terms of its age, elusiveness and complexity – to these pupils? The answer is because I believed in the validity of what Brian Cox has described as the *cultural heritage* model of English, one which 'emphasises the responsibility of schools to lead children to an appreciation of those works of literature that have been widely regarded as amongst the finest in the language' (Cox 1991: 21).

Why had I been so pleased, and at the same time, exasperated by Alan's momentary engagement with *Mariana*? Because I found it thrilling that a young man of uncertain future, about to start his adult life in a run-down, post-industrial northern town, could, for a moment, through the medium of literature, reach across boundaries of time, class and culture in order to try to understand what somebody else's loneliness might feel like. I believed that by achieving this, Alan was experiencing what Cox describes as the *personal growth* model of English: 'A "personal growth" view focuses on the child: it emphasises the relationship between language and learning in the individual child, and *the role of literature in developing children's imaginative and aesthetic lives*' (Cox 1991: 22, my italics).

In the context of this *personal growth* model, I was gratified, too, to think that Alan had appreciated the artifice of literature: the ways in which meanings can resonate at a sub-textual level; the playful ambiguity of metaphor, pun, allusion; the fact that a piece of writing can have a hidden agenda and is not always to be taken at face value.

Both these models which influenced my decision to teach *Mariana* belong to a tradition reaching back at least two hundred years. Romantic poets like Wordsworth and Shelley would have endorsed this privileging of literature in the classroom. Neither of them would have been surprised to know that engagement with a poem had helped a young student to articulate a sense of empathy. For Shelley, Alan's response to *Mariana* would have offered confirmation that: 'Poetry strengthens the faculty which is the organ of the moral nature of man, in the same manner as exercise strengthens the limb' (in Mathieson 1975: 41).

Nineteenth-century reformers like Matthew Arnold endorsed the Romantic position. The more the social structures of Britain were shaken by the industrial, scientific, ethical and political changes of the period, the more education in general – and the study of literature in particular – were invested with a near-religious capacity to transform and redeem society (McGuinn 2002). Writing half a century after Shelley's death, Matthew Arnold forcefully reasserted the latter's claims for poetry:

> We should conceive of poetry worthily, and more highly than it has been the custom to conceive of it ... More and more mankind will discover that we have to turn to poetry to interpret life for us to console us, to sustain us. Without poetry, our science will appear incomplete; and most of what now passes with us for religion and philosophy, will be replaced by poetry.
>
> (in Mathieson 1975: 40)

The twentieth century brought even greater need for Arnold's 'interpretation', 'sustenance' and 'consolation'. This was an age of mass movements – mass destruction on the battlefields of the two World Wars or in the concentration camps of Nazi-occupied Europe and the Communist Soviet Union; the increasing alienation of human beings from their labour through mass industrialisation with its attendant disruption of age-old agrarian cultures and environments; ever more sophisticated attempts by the forces of the mass media and by economic or political agencies to manipulate whole populations on a national, continental and even global scale.

As the power of these forces grew, so the urge to turn to literature and the arts as a source of spiritual, imaginative and creative nourishment for the beleaguered human individual became more urgent. In 1921, for example, the Newbolt Report re-affirmed the power of literature to repair a social fabric grievously damaged by the ravages of the First World War:

> We claim that no personality can be complete, can see life steadily and see it whole, without that unifying influence, that purifying of the emotions which art and literature can alone bestow. It follows then from what we have said above that the bulk of our people, of whatever class, are unconsciously living starved existences, that one of the richest fields of our spiritual being is left uncultivated – not indeed barren, for the weeds of literature have never been so prolific as in our day.
>
> (HMSO 1921: 257)

Of all those who have championed this position, few can have had a more significant influence upon twentieth-century teachers than the group of academics who, dominated by such figures as I. A. Richards and F. R. Leavis, established in the early decades of the century what was to become known as the 'Cambridge School' of English. Through such seminal texts as *Principles of Literary Criticism* (1935 [1924]), Richards argued that rigorous training in the sensitive and disciplined reading of literary texts could help individuals to hone their sense of moral awareness by gaining access to what were perceived to be the beautiful and timeless moral truths enshrined in works of great literature. Viewed from this perspective, the act of reading assumes a moral, almost religious, quality. Its purpose was to protect the human spirit against the cultural disintegration which Richards observed in contemporary society and to offer a countervailing capacity for informed and discriminating judgement powerful enough to resist the pressure for stereotypical, shallow responses typified, for Richards, by the rise of the mass media:

For many reasons standards are much more in need of defence than they used to be. It is perhaps premature to envisage a collapse of values, a transvaluation by which popular taste replaces trained discrimination. Yet commercialism has done stranger things ... Sinister potentialities of cinema and loud speaker ... best sellers, magazine verses ... music hall songs ... are decreasing in merit ... At present bad literature, bad art, the cinema etc., are an influence of the first importance in fixing immature and actually inapplicable attitudes to most things.

(Richards 1935: 36, 202)

For Leavis – a witness to the rise of Fascism throughout 1930s Europe – the expertise with which the Nazis manipulated the mass media for propaganda purposes lent a terrible authority to Richards' warnings from the previous decade:

The social and cultural disintegration that has accompanied the development of the vast modern machine is destroying what should have been the control, and leaves a terrifying apparatus of propaganda ready to the hands of the more or less subtle, more or less conscious, more or less direct, emulators of Hitler and his accomplices. What is to forestall or check them? ... Without an intelligent, educated and morally responsible public, political programmes can do nothing to arrest the process of disintegration.

(Leavis 1943: 118)

Leavis' famous rallying-cry – 'discriminate and resist' (Leavis 1943: 3) – struck a responsive chord, not only for the generations of students who studied under him, but also, perforce, for the pupils to whom those students-turned-teachers later disseminated his ideas, particularly through the mid years of the century. So potent is the legacy of Leavis' belief that the engagement with what he would unhesitatingly describe as 'great' literature can refine the critical faculties, enhance one's own command of language and nourish both spirit and imagination, that the study of canonical texts is enshrined by law in today's National Curriculum.

The influence of academics such as Richards and Leavis upon the *cultural heritage* model of English represents one contemporary manifestation of the Romantic tradition which informed my attempt to introduce Alan to Tennyson's poetry in that recent GCSE lesson described at the beginning of the chapter. There is, however, a second branch of the tradition which, while sympathetic to much of what Leavis says about the capacity of the arts and literature to embed the individual within a sustaining culture, shifts the emphasis from receiving to making.

Mathieson (1975) has described how, at the start of the twentieth century, educators in England became increasingly receptive to a constructivist paradigm of learning, one which, drawing upon the works of European and American theorists such as Rousseau, Froebel and Dewey, placed the individual at the centre of the learning experience, celebrating each person's unique motivation and ability to negotiate meanings for themselves through active and incremental engagement with the world around them. Caldwell Cook was one of the most significant of these early English champions of creativity. In *The Play Way* – a text which was to have an important influence upon the Newbolt Report cited earlier – he wrote: 'Let us remember that without interest there is no learning, and since the child's interest is all in play it is necessary whatever the method in hand that the method be a play method' (Cook 1917: 3).

In the mid years of the century, English theorists like David Holbrook and, later, John Dixon (whose 1967 publication *Growth Through English* proved particularly influential) were instrumental in developing and consolidating the *personal growth* model of English described earlier in the chapter. Echoing and redirecting the thoughts of I. A. Richards described earlier, Dixon suggested that: 'In ordering and composing situations that in some way symbolise life as we know it, we bring order and composure to our inner selves' (Dixon 1967: 20).

Holbrook argued that English should be located firmly within the creative arts. Like Dixon, he believed that the purpose of true literacy was to effect the integration of the whole personality on a cognitive, emotional and, crucially, a psychic level. By achieving this, genuinely creative English teachers could help their pupils forge links between the cultural life of the individual and the cultural life of the society in which he or she lives:

> Creative activity can thus become a gateway to the richness of civilisation which the teacher draws from the body of English poetry, as opportunity arises, to find immediately relevant examples to nourish the inward progress of each pupil as he strives towards insight.
>
> (Holbrook 1968: 13)

This movement in English teaching achieved its fullest expression in the 1960s and 1970s, first at the famous Anglo-American seminar on the teaching of English held at Dartmouth College, New Hampshire in 1966[1] and subsequently in the pages of *A Language for Life* – otherwise known as The Bullock Report of 1975 – which helped to set the English teaching agenda for the following decade. As in the case of *cultural heritage*, the legacy of the *personal growth* model is still potent enough for its importance to have been granted statutory recognition in the National Curriculum. Its influence can be felt whenever pupils are invited to create oral and written texts which draw upon the powers of the imagination or which help them – in the words of Holbrook again – to establish 'links between the civilisation which is growing in each child' and 'the inheritance of civilisation on the shelves of libraries and in the English tongue itself' (Holbrook 1968: 14).

Surveys consistently suggest that both the *cultural heritage* and, particularly, the *personal growth* models of English are highly valued by teachers (Goodwyn 1992; Hardman and Williamson 1993; Hardman 2001).

When I walked into that GCSE Literature classroom to teach Tennyson's *Mariana*, I did so with a sense of confidence borne of the knowledge that my choice of text and teaching style was endorsed by a venerable pedagogic tradition which had, for over a century,[2] received increasing support from the educational establishment and which was endorsed by my teaching colleagues. Alan, however, remained unimpressed and unengaged. He is not alone. In fact, as Stevens, citing Hirsch, demonstrates again in Chapter 6: if called to account for its contribution to the development of literacy, the advocates of this curriculum would have some uncomfortable questions to answer. In 1999, the Department for Education and Employment Report *A Fresh Start* offered some sombre reflections about standards of adult literacy and numeracy, as these opening remarks from the Chair of the working group, Sir Claus Moser, made clear:

> We have found that people are staggered when one confronts them with the basic facts about literacy and numeracy, and rightly so. It is staggering that over the years millions of children have been leaving school hardly able to read and write, and that today millions of adults have the same problems . . . the stark facts are all too clear. Roughly 20% of adults – that is perhaps as many as 7 million people – have more or less severe problems with basic skills, in particular with what is generally called 'functional literacy' and 'functional numeracy'.
>
> (DfEE 1999: 2)

Findings like these oblige us to question the efficacy of a literacy curriculum based upon a creative engagement with literature. But why should an educational enterprise endorsed by so many visionary thinkers over the past two hundred years, one so committed to the life-affirming principle of helping individuals to find their personal voice and to negotiate a cultural identity for themselves in an increasingly unstable, authoritarian and impersonal world, appear to achieve so little success and be met with the sullen disengagement typified by Alan's response in the GCSE Literature lesson?

Stevens has already begun to explore, in Chapter 2, the reasons why creativity may fail to flourish in the English classroom. I want to pursue that issue now by returning to my lesson on Tennyson's *Mariana*. In an attempt to be true to David Holbrook's principles of creative response,

I had invited Alan and his classmates to 'story-board' key moments from the poem. When I collected the work in, I noticed that one girl had drawn a picture of a woman staring out at an urban landscape from the window of a high-rise tower block. Surprised to see such an image drawn in response to a poem which seemed to me to be so evidently located in a rural setting, I asked the pupil to tell me which line from the poem her picture illustrated. The reply came without hesitation: *She drew her casement-curtain by,/And glanced athwart the glooming flats.*

For Tennyson, 'flats' meant desolate Lincolnshire marshland. For this fifteen-year-old Yorkshire girl reading the poem over 150 years after it was written, the word meant the kind of run-down dwelling to be found in countless inner city areas throughout the north of England. Looking back now on that apparently inconsequential – perhaps even humorous – classroom incident, it seems to me to be charged with ideological and peda-gogical significance. In fact, I would argue that it encapsulates the key issue with which this chapter is concerned.

When that Yorkshire girl drew her picture of the 'glooming flats', she was trying to reach out, sincerely and openly, from the world of her culture, identity and language to a wider world represented by what Leavis would call the 'great tradition' of canonical literature. Viewing this exchange from the *personal growth* perspective advocated by Dixon or Holbrook – one which regards literacy as being concerned with 'the energies of the inner world and the whole personality' and in which English as a creative art has a fundamentally important role to play in that it enables us to 'relate our inward world to the outer world by metaphor' (Holbrook 1968: 6, 5) – this pupil's response to the poem becomes particularly significant. If, as Holbrook argues, creative engagements such as this girl's picture 'refer not only to outward objective referents, but to aspects of the subjective life which always colour our attitude to and our perception of subjective reality' (Holbrook 1968: 9), then the story-board image becomes much more than a quick bit of art-work produced at teacher's behest on a dull Friday afternoon. It is as if Tennyson and the fifteen-year-old Yorkshire girl are in dialogue about the psychic impact of desolation, abandonment and hopelessness upon the human spirit. For him, it is symbolised by the image of a woman imprisoned in a decaying 'moated grange' haunted by memo-ries and ghosts and surrounded by desolate marshland. For her, it is symbolised by a woman imprisoned in a decaying high-rise apartment set in a desolate urban landscape.

How the 'mindful teacher' – as Stevens puts it – manages this key moment of transition between two cultures is crucial. One approach would be to dismiss the picture (and the pupil) with a laugh, taking the opportu-nity to lecture the class about the importance of place in Tennyson's poetry and thinking, perhaps, that the incident might make a brief and amusing anecdote to relate in the staff room at the end of the day. Would this matter? The Leeds-born poet Tony Harrison thinks so. In his poem *Them & [uz]* he recalls a similar classroom incident in which his attempt to respond to a canonical literary text – Keats' *Ode to a Nightingale* – was met with the kind of negative response I have just conjectured:

---

4 words only of *mi 'art aches* and . . . 'Mine's broken,
you barbarian, T.W.' *He* was nicely spoken.
'Can't have our glorious heritage done to death.'

I played the Drunken Porter in *Macbeth.*

'Poetry's the speech of kings'. You're one of those
Shakespeare gives the comic bits to: prose.

(Harrison 1978: 20)

The Russian theorist Mikhail Bakhtin would have regarded the incident described here by Harrison as a classic manifestation of a fundamental tension which sees language as continually: 'pulled in opposite directions: centripetally, towards the unitary centre provided by a notion of a "national language"; and centrifugally, towards the various languages which actually constitute the apparent but false unity of a national language' (Dentith 1995: 37).

Viewed from this perspective, the experience of initiation becomes not the life-affirming and liberating finding of one's individual voice within the cultural 'choir' which Holbrook envisioned, but actually an example of what Paolo Freire (1990) might have described as 'cultural imperialism' through the enforcement of one linguistic form upon another.

The comprehensive-school girl who risks ridicule for misinterpreting the meaning of the word 'flats', the grammar-school boy who actually suffers ridicule for reciting Keats in a Leeds accent – both could be said to 'live their oppression by viewing themselves from the perspective of the way others view them' (McLaren and Lankshear 1994: 5). Suddenly, Keats' *Ode to a Nightingale* and Tennyson's *Mariana* are transformed from wonderful, engaging, mysterious works of art into some kind of measuring device by which to gauge the perceived linguistic and cultural inadequacies of others. A politically engaged critic like Pierre Bourdieu (1991) would take the analogy further by suggesting that both these texts are sites of cultural and symbolic power to which the teacher, as 'gatekeeper', allows access to those who have the necessary 'cultural capital' to buy their way in. Middle-class children – whose values and discursive practices are privileged by the school system – are far more likely, Bourdieu would argue, to gain entry to these sites of power than a girl who only knows one meaning of the word 'flats' or a boy who pronounces 'heart' without the aitch.

Tony Harrison cannot resist making the point that the revered canonical author of *Ode to a Nightingale* was, himself, a Cockney who would probably have recited his poem in an accent even more objectionable to the 'nicely spoken' grammar-school teacher than his own. It is deeply ironic that the writers who comprise what I have described as the *cultural heritage* strand of the 'Romantic' curriculum – provocative and often radical thinkers like Shakespeare or Blake – should have been 'hijacked' by the political establishment as a means of asserting ideological power. This is, however, what has happened. When the National Curriculum was still at the planning stage, it was from the political Right that the heaviest pressure to privilege a *cultural heritage* model of English came. In 1988, for example, Sheila Lawlor, Deputy Director of the Centre for Policy Studies, argued that, in the planned statutory curriculum, 'pupils should be acquainted with the recognised classics of English literature as a first step towards understanding the literary heritage. It [the statutory core curriculum] will expect pupils to learn by heart certain passages of literature, and to read carefully certain books' (Lawlor 1988: 23).

These would include 'at least one play by Shakespeare and a variety of poetry, including some written before this century'. Lawlor also suggested that pupils should 'know by heart several further passages from the authorised version of the Bible; a short speech or soliloquy by Shakespeare; several short poems (or extracts from longer poems) by Milton, Pope, Wordsworth, *Keats or Tennyson*' (Lawlor, 1988: 28, my italics).

In the years which followed, right-wing politicians skilfully manipulated the discourse surrounding canonical texts so that it became difficult to discuss them in any other contexts than those of standards, authority and national identity. Shortly before Sheila Lawlor published her recommendations for the *cultural heritage* model of English, a senior Conservative politician hinted at a link between deviance from what Bakhtin would call normative, standardised language (the language equated with the literary canon) and criminal behaviour:

> We've allowed so many standards to slip . . . Teachers weren't bothering to teach kids to spell and to punctuate properly . . . if you allow standards to slip to the stage where good English is no better than bad English, where students turn up filthy . . . at school . . . All those things tend to cause people to have no standards at all, and once you lose standards then there's no imperative to stay out of crime.
>
> (in Bain 1991: 12)

And only a few years after that, his political compatriot, a man who at the time was Secretary of State for Education, made the tentative link between standards and canonical texts explicit (while at the same time unconsciously and ironically underscoring Bourdieu's point about 'cultural capital'): 'The sooner children master the basic skills and become confident users of standard English the sooner they can enjoy the pleasures and rewards of our literature' (DES/WO 1993: 71).

John Patten may have been clear in his own mind about whom that personal pronoun was meant to include; but its use might not be quite as unproblematic as he supposed. Whose literature, precisely, is covered by the word 'our'? I decided to put this question to the test by inviting a comprehensive-school class of fourteen-year-old pupils studying for their English Standard Assessment Tests (SATs) to tell me what they knew about the kinds of canonical poetic texts beloved of Matthew Arnold, the members of the Newbolt Committee, F. R. Leavis and John Patten himself. I asked the twenty-six pupils if they could name a poet who had written before the famous National Curriculum watershed year of 1914. Twelve pupils offered William Shakespeare; the other fourteen said they could not think of anybody. I also asked the class if they could name a poem written before 1914. Nineteen pupils said they could not do this. Of the seven who did provide a title, two offered a nursery rhyme (*The Grand Old Duke of York*) and one suggested a play (Shakespeare's *Romeo and Juliet*). Only four pupils actually cited a pre-1914 poem: one mentioned the medieval Latin work, *Carmina Burana* (written in Germany) and three named the Scottish ballad *Lord Ullin's Daughter* by Thomas Campbell (1777–1844) – not a work which Leavis might have cited as one of the finest examples of the 'great tradition' but perhaps something the class had studied recently in English.

I also asked the pupils what they imagined a poem written before 1914 might be like. Not a single answer suggested a response which could be construed as in any way positive: there was no indication of excitement or curiosity or anticipation. Four pupils suggested that such poems would be about 'love' (in a pejorative, overly sentimental sense of the word); three said the themes would probably be 'sad' or 'lonely'; other, single, respondents suggested that such poems would be 'uninteresting', 'not funny', 'sombre', 'lacking in sense' – and even 'poorly punctuated'! The main pattern of response focused upon a perception that poetry written before 1914 would be very different linguistically from current modes of discourse and therefore alien and hard to understand. Eleven respondents said that they expected such poems to be written in 'old English' [*sic*] or 'old language'; two more used the phrase 'different dialects' and another mentioned 'unknown words'.

I do not wish to make overblown claims for this very small convenience sample taken from one particular class in one particular school on one particular day. Perhaps the respondents were simply feigning ignorance of a curriculum model they had known all their school lives in order to shock the visitor who was asking them strange questions about their English lessons. If this were the case, however, the pupils arrived at the decision individually, for they had no opportunity for prior discussion or collusion.

The respondents to this questionnaire attend a rural comprehensive school in a decidedly mono-ethnic, white community. If these pupils claim that they find canonical texts unattractive and alien, what might be expected from those who come from different home cultures, or for whom English is not a first language? Thirty miles away from the school in which I conducted my survey, there is another Year 9 SAT examination class with a very different ethnic mix. Of its twenty-three members, nine pupils are white; four are Pakistani; three are African-Caribbean mixed race; two are Bengali; two are Asian mixed race and the other three are African-Caribbean, Chinese and Philippine respectively.

Research suggests that the prognosis for these pupils is not good. A Topic Paper published by the DfEE in 2000 drew attention to 'a clear pattern of continuous under achievement for certain ethnic groups which starts in early education, continues through further and higher education, and persists in the labour market' (DfEE 2000: 1).

Bangladeshi, Black and Pakistani pupils particularly, the Paper noted, are losing out to their white peers at every life-stage: in early years education; at GCSE; in full-time employment. Black Caribbean boys appear to be the most disadvantaged of all. The explanation for this offered by the Topic Paper brings forcibly to mind Bourdieu's comments about the ideological power of 'cultural capital':

> Once at secondary school, Black Caribbean boys may be subjected to a greater risk of underachievement compared to whites because of a combination of regular truancy, low teacher expectations, conflict and tension with teachers and a high relative probability of being permanently excluded.
>
> (DfEE 2000: 4)

Reading statements like this from an official government agency, one can understand the passion behind this recent outburst from the writers of a key textbook on contemporary educational studies: 'The influence of ethnic difference on levels of achievement in state schooling systems remains one of the great scandals of contemporary western-style education systems' (Bartlett *et al.* 2001: 198).

Black Caribbean boys who – by the DfEE's own admission – find 'few role models in school' and whose 'resistance' to the dominant ideological power of the educational system too often precipitates 'serious disciplinary responses such as exclusion' (DfEE 2000: 5), may well feel that

Shakespeare's *Henry V, Macbeth* and *Twelfth Night*, or Robert Louis Stevenson's *Treasure Island*,[3] have little to say to them; and they might well ask, too, whether their voices and their stories are included in John Patten's definition of 'our' literature.

One of the consequences of that binding of the *cultural heritage* model of English to notions of identity which accompanied the foundation of the National Curriculum in the late 1980s and early 1990s was that the global claims of the language were largely ignored. Even the latest, 1999 version of the statutory requirements for Literature in the National Curriculum at Key Stages 3 and 4 insists on the study of two plays by Shakespeare as well as of works of fiction and poetry drawn from a prescriptive list of pre-1914 writers, most of whom are male and English. Whereas these works are printed in bold type, as though to emphasise the fact that they have the weight of the law behind them, those by writers from other parts of the world who have chosen to work in English are afforded the lower status of exemplar texts and are represented in an appropriately insipid grey (DfEE 1999: 35, 36). How adequate is this model of a literature curriculum for life in a world where over 300 million people outside the United Kingdom speak English as their first language and a further billion use it as a second tongue (Ash 2000: 97)?

The nineteenth- and twentieth-century proponents of the *cultural heritage* curriculum prepared the conditions whereby right-wing politicians were later able to link the debate about the study of literature to notions of standards, identity and correctness, through their insistence that qualitative judgements could and should be made concerning the relative value of different forms of cultural expression. The 'art and literature' which the Newbolt Committee envisioned 'purifying ... the emotions' of a ravaged, post-war society were much more rarified entities than the 'weeds of literature' which they perceived to be growing so prolifically among the 'bulk of our people' (HMSO 1921: 257). Leavis and Thompson developed this argument even more forcefully in their important text, *Culture and Environment*. For them, art and literature provided the means by which English teachers might cultivate 'taste and sensibility' in their pupils and thus help them resist what were perceived to be the malign, debasing influences of the mass media:

> Many teachers of English who have become interested in the possibilities of training taste and sensibility must have been troubled by accompanying doubts. What effect can such training have against the multitudinous counterinfluences – films, newspapers, advertising – indeed the whole world outside the classroom? Yet the very conditions that make literary education look so desperate are those which make it more important than ever before; for in a world of this kind – and

a world that changes so rapidly – it is on literary tradition that the office of maintaining continuity must rest.

(Leavis and Thompson 1933: 1)

As Masterman (1985: 39) has pointed out, statements such as these belong to a 'long history of "respectable fears" about the moral corruption of working people through their predilection for debased amusements' – a tradition which Pearson (1983: 33) sees stretching back to the days of the 'cheap theatres and penny-gaffs of early Victorian England' and beyond. Masterman's introduction of class into the argument is important here. By keeping popular art-forms off the statutory lists of the National Curriculum, the *cultural heritage* model risks the charge of legitimising and privileging certain forms of artistic expression at the expense of others and thus, as Bourdieu, Bakhtin or Freire might argue, declaring other ways of knowing and experiencing the world as inferior if not invalid – with all the consequences such acts of categorisation have for those who live and express their identity through what are perceived to be marginalised forms of communication:

if you are one of the world's population who speaks a non-prestige version of your 'national' language or indeed don't speak that language at all, you will know the sharp and sometimes bitterly conflictual tensions that surround every word you speak.

(Dentith 1995: 37)

Mikhail Bakhtin argued that certain kinds of discourse could be described as 'authoritative'. In the words of Harold Rosen, an authoritative discourse demands 'our unconditional allegiance – permits no play within its borders, no gradual or flexible transitions, no creative stylising variants. It is indissolubly fused with authority. All is inertia and calcification' (Rosen 1992: 127).

How many pupils in our schools today feel, like Alan, that the major works of the *cultural heritage* curriculum are 'authoritative texts', designed to initiate them – not into a life-enhancing and creative dialogue between the self and the culture into which it is born – but into a sense of inadequacy and compliance to which the only possible responses are sullen obedience or the establishment of a countervailing sub-culture of resistance (Bowles and Gintis 1976; Willis 1979)?

When Alan suggested that a knowledge of Tennyson's *Mariana* would be of little use to him on his uncle's building-site, he was arguing a pedagogical case which has, since the 1970s onwards, mounted an increasingly potent challenge to the *cultural heritage* and *personal growth* models which form the twin pillars of the Romantic literacy curriculum. The kinds of discourses encouraged by these two models are deeply reflective, even self-centred. Pupils might explore their response to the theme of sight and blindness in *King Lear*, for example, or meditate – almost in the Wordsworthian sense of recalling emotion in tranquillity – upon some personal experience which has had a significant impact upon their lives, or, again, exercise their imaginations by writing fantastical narratives. As early as 1958, the humorist Ronald Searle satirised this latter approach through the words of his comic creation, Nigel Molesworth, who sums up his experience of writing lessons at St Custard's Preparatory School thus: 'For essays english [*sic*] masters give us weedy things like – a trip in a space ship, my favourite machine gun (Willans and Searle 1985: 35).

The dominant genre encountered by Molesworth in his English lessons was that of narrative fiction. Surveying the development of English teaching almost half a century later, Andrews (2001: 45) noted that narrative continued to extend its grip upon the English curriculum long after Molesworth left St Custard's: 'In the late 1970s and 1980s, in the wake of studies in narrative form by linguists, anthropologists and literary and cultural critics, narrative established itself as the orthodoxy at the foundation of English work in schools.'

Alan's rejection of the work associated with the study of Tennyson's *Mariana* has been endorsed, particularly, by sociolinguists. Thirteen years ago, when the National Curriculum was first gaining momentum, Peter Medway complained about the absence, from the school curriculum, of what he called 'perlocutionary level' language. At the perlocutionary level, Medway argued, 'we use our utterances as social acts to influence others, to soothe, threaten, impel, amuse, or to make people do things or stop them doing things' (Medway 1989: 28–29).

Pupils engaged in an exploration of the *cultural heritage* and *personal growth* models of English, Medway's argument ran, would have little opportunity to use language as a means of effecting change in the world: 'They will not cancel an order, order an arrest, make a recipe, move supplies from one place to another, meet someone from a train or engage in civil disobedience.' Medway concluded his article somewhat bleakly: 'Language in schools, it seems, has always, since antiquity, been divorced from action' (Medway 1989: 30).

This argument opens up a compelling new line of political attack upon the Romantic literacy curriculum. Viewed from the perspective of Jürgen Habermas and the critical theorists of the Frankfurt School, a curriculum that encourages its students to preoccupy themselves with the study and production of texts which carry little authority or capacity to effect change within or beyond the school gates, is simply embedding within the consciousness of young people – particularly those from the most disempowered sections of society – important ideological messages about compliance and passivity (Young 1989).

remembered as a 'kind of force-feeding' – Seamus Heaney recalled that it was only when memory enabled him to make the links described here by Spender that he really started to engage with those texts:

> I . . . knew the whole of Keats's ode 'To Autumn' but the only line that was luminous then was 'To bend with apples the mossed cottage trees', because my uncle had a small orchard where the old apple trees were sleeved in a soft green moss.
>
> (Heaney 1980: 26)

By asserting the claims of the individual reading voice in the engagement between literary text and audience, Rosenblatt gave validity and authority to the kind of personal response to Keats' *mossed cottage tree* described here by Heaney or revealed in my GCSE pupil's interpretation of Tennyson's *glooming flats*. Rosenblatt's position is problematic, however. Like John Dixon – who, in the quotation offered earlier in the chapter, argued that 'we bring order and composure to our inner selves' by 'ordering and composing situations that in some way symbolise life as we know it' – she is investing too much faith in the capacity of the individual consciousness to act as a supreme, rational arbiter of meanings.

Take the poem overleaf as an example. It was written over thirty years ago by Geoffrey Hill, a writer working very consciously within what the Cambridge School would have regarded as the great canonical tradition of English literature. The poem provides a graphic illustration of an artist attempting to use the medium of language to bring 'order and composure' to one of humanity's most horrifying experiences – the Holocaust.

Seamus Heaney – a poet who has also attempted to confront the dark forces in human nature through his art – framed the creative challenge faced here by Hill in terms of a question borrowed from Shakespeare's *Sonnet 65: How with this rage shall beauty hold a plea?* 'My answer is', Heaney suggested, quoting his fellow Irish poet William Butler Yeats, 'by offering "befitting emblems of adversity"' (Heaney 1980: 57).

For me, the 'emblems' chosen by Hill to represent the horror of the Nazi genocide are powerful ones: the 'Zyklon' gas crystals used to perpetrate the act of mass murder; the 'leather' worn by the camp guards. The counter-balancing 'emblems' of beauty are equally potent, I feel: vines fattening in the September sun and roses flaking on the wall evoke the natural, timeless rhythms of growth and fertility which the ten-year-old Holocaust victim – whose own short and vulnerable life has flaked from the wall as easily and as unnoticed as a dying flower – will never live to enjoy. Most moving for me is Hill's use of the seemingly mundane adjective 'harmless' in front of the noun 'fires'. It seems to force the reader to recall those anything but harmless concentration camp flames which cremated the bodies of so many millions of victims. Recalling Stevens' quote from Kureishi in Chapter 2,

SEPTEMBER SONG
born 19.6.32 – deported 24.9.42

Undesirable you may have been, untouchable
you were not. Not forgotten
or passed over at the proper time.

As estimated, you died. Things marched,
sufficient, to that end.
Just so much Zyklon and leather, patented
terror, so many routine cries.

(I have made
an elegy for myself it
is true)

September fattens on vines. Roses
flake from the wall. The smoke
of harmless fires drifts to my eyes.

This is plenty. This is more than enough.

(Hill 1968: 19)

I find that one of the greatest strengths of this magnificent poem is the way that it confronts an evil sustained by noise – the noise of the hate-fuelled chanting of a racist mob or the overblown, demented hectoring of a Fascist rally – with words that are quiet, pared-down, patient, allusive and elusive.

I have offered here a reading of Geoffrey Hill's *September Song* which attempts to demonstrate the characteristics of Louise Rosenblatt's 'personal response'. Writing in the first person, I have tried to bring to bear all those qualities – 'personality traits, memories of past events' and the rest – described in the quotation cited earlier: my experience of reading texts and watching films about the Holocaust; the visit I paid to the crematoria of Dachau when I was fourteen, my previous engagement with poetry and so on. But who is to say that this response is more valid than one which, drawing from equally personal well-springs of interpretation, constructed a very different reading of the poem? A reading which, for example, attributed no connotative effect to the phrase 'harmless fires'; or suggested that the final statement of the poem is an expression of complacency; or even – worst of all – interpreted the first seven lines literally? Are we to say that the right of each individual to impose whatever meanings they wish upon the text is sacrosanct?

This is where the post-structuralist theories of reading which have exercised such a seismic influence on English studies over the past half century demand to be taken into account. They challenge the authority of the personal response by demonstrating that meanings are not fixed for ever but are actually negotiated by authors, texts and readers who are, themselves, embedded within particular political, temporal, social and cultural contexts (Peim 1993). Viewed from this perspective, the questions asked of literary texts shift from the self-referential (*What can this text teach me about myself?*) or reverential (*What can this text teach me about life?*) or authoritarian (*How can this text help me gain access to the dominant culture in which I live?*) – to something more politically engaged, more bracingly egalitarian, more receptive to pluralist interpretations. They might include the following:

- Who is communicating and why?
- What type of text is it?
- How is it produced?
- How do we know what it means?
- Who receives it and what sense do they make of it?
- How does it present its subject?

(Bowker 1991: 6)

Questions such as these mean that it is no longer possible for any literary work – whether it be by William Shakespeare or Geoffrey Hill – to assume as an automatic, uncontested right, the status of 'authoritative text'. For many, this might be a matter of regret. Personally, I believe that Hill's poem speaks so powerfully and movingly about the Holocaust that if I were called upon to create a canon of essential literary works, *September Song* would be at the heart of it. Similarly, much as I might deplore – abhor, even – interpretations of this poem which ran counter to the one I offered above, I cannot deny the fact that it is possible to construct multiple readings of texts nor that one might choose to 'read against' the meanings I have suggested here.

The legacy which post-structuralism has bequeathed to literary texts is the seemingly harsh injunction that they must make their own way in the world and 'fight their own corner'. They must earn rather than demand authority. To ask of *September Song* a question such as *How do we know what it means?* is to force a re-examination of deeply rooted assumptions which we might otherwise – lazily or even arrogantly perhaps – have simply assumed to be 'common sense'. If we are to answer that question, we have to scrutinise, of course, the reading practices by which we make sense of poetry – our understanding of such devices as metaphor and metonomy, for example, or the capacity for rhythm to 'persuade' where reason 'convinces', as the poet C. H. Sisson so memorably put it (Schmidt 1980: 25). But more than that, we have to ask ourselves what it is about the political, moral and social values that we as a democratic society share which unite us behind the reading of *September Song* described earlier. Why would we, as a society, find an aberrant reading of that text morally repugnant? Is it even safe to assume that we would find it morally repugnant? What safeguards should we put in place in order to ensure that such aberrant readings never gain a dominant position in our political and cultural order?

Finding answers to each of the six questions listed above takes our engagement with literary texts far beyond the realms of personal response and into a political world where competing power discourses struggle for domination. The implications of these challenges for the pedagogy of English teachers committed to a Romantic agenda will be the focus of my next chapter and will be explored again by Stevens in Chapter 6.

4 The challenge of 'instrumental rationality'

How with this rage shall beauty hold a plea?
(William Shakespeare, *Sonnet 65*)

Perhaps the most pressing attack upon the Romantic position is the one voiced by my pupil Alan in that GCSE lesson on Tennyson's *Mariana* described in the previous chapter – the plea for what Jürgen Habermas described as 'instrumental rationality' (Habermas 1970). Alan did not want to read Victorian poetry anymore because he regarded its concerns and its discourses as irrelevant to the concerns and discourses of the working adult world he was about to enter.

Alan is in powerful company. In 1976, the then Labour Prime Minister, James Callaghan, initiated what was to become known as the 'Great Debate' on education when he called the service to public account: 'I take it that no one claims exclusive rights in this field [of education]. Public interest is strong and legitimate and will be satisfied. We spend £6 billion a year on education, so there will be discussion' (Callaghan 1976: 332).

Callaghan's words offered an implicit threat to the Romantic educational agenda and its quasi-religious belief in the powers of the liberal arts to restore and even transform the social fabric. Proponents of that agenda had, for over a century, demanded teachers of exceptional spirit and personality. In the words of the nineteenth-century educationalist, Henry Sidgwick, the 'schoolmaster' was to be nothing less than a 'missionary of culture' (Sidgwick 1868: 106). The burden of expectation was placed most heavily upon English teachers. As Mathieson puts it:

> At every stage of the subject's growth, during which new hopes have been invested in it as a liberalising force, fresh demands have been made for inspirational teachers. In response to what they have seen as a worsening cultural crisis, educationalists have recurrently called for exceptional teachers to face unsympathetic conditions in the schools and the 'forces' of modern urban society.
>
> (Mathieson 1975: 12)

In the early decades of the twentieth century, the educationalist Edward Blishen was taught by just such an 'inspirational' teacher who appeared to have come straight from the Romantic mould:

> Now I had passed gratefully, for English, into the care of a Welshman, Williams. He was a tiny man, some childish illness had left him small, reared on music and poetry, with an Oxford voice that at moments of excitement became a Welsh one. We measured his disciplinary temper by his slide into sing-song. He had the best of qualifications for teaching English – a great feeling for words and for what they could do. He taught English, in the first place, by speaking it richly; off the point, very often off the point, but always with vivacity. With him we never reached the end of a set book.
>
> (Blishen 1978: 133)

Williams represents many of the strengths traditionally associated with the Romantic English teacher – and also the qualities which Callaghan most deeply distrusted. Williams was charismatic, inspirational, a gifted practitioner of the arts he loved; but he was also a maverick, a kind of Nietzschean 'free spirit' who went his own way and defied the conventions of his school by improvising his lessons and ignoring the obligations of examination and syllabus.

By opening the so-called 'secret garden' of education to public scrutiny, Callaghan made it possible for those who had no truck with the idea that English teaching might be some mysterious priestly vocation to go on the offensive. Writing on the eve of the National Curriculum in 1988, Sheila Lawlor led the assault:

> The teaching of English today – even more so than of other subjects – suffers from too many ambitious but vague aims, and from a neglect of the importance of basic skills and knowledge. That is why pupils leave school unable to read precisely and confidently, and to write clear, correct English.
>
> (Lawlor 1988: 6)

Under the Conservative administrations of the late twentieth century, even education ministers felt able to join in the attack on the kind of professionalism represented by Mr Williams: 'Advice of the professionals is not always sound. Was it not professional advice that gave us the secret garden [of the hidden curriculum], that gave us education without grammar and spelling?' (in McGuinn 1994: 135).

The 'delivery' – as the current jargon has it – of Lawlor's 'basic skills and knowledge' had less need of improvisational brilliance than of the thorough, painstaking implementation of a pre-ordained set of quantifiable educational targets. As Stevens has observed earlier in the book, the three decades which have followed Callaghan's 'Ruskin College Speech' have witnessed a move – through the introduction of a National Curriculum and of Standard Assessment Tests – towards ever-increasing state control of what is taught in schools and how the effectiveness of that teaching might be measured. The role of the English teacher has moved accordingly, it could be argued, from autonomous professional to something more akin to that of the technician, where responsibility for curriculum implementation and assessment is accompanied not by corresponding rights but by a series of monitoring and policing procedures designed to keep teachers continually on the defensive and in a state of 'manufactured anxiety' (Hargreaves and Goodson 1996: 11).

Nothing, perhaps, demonstrates more forcibly this perceived change in the English teacher's role than the language chosen by educational policy makers to address the teaching profession. When the Bullock Committee published its seminal blueprint for English teaching, *A Language for Life*, in 1975, the tone it adopted was thoughtful, hesitant and conciliatory:

> The solution does not lie in a few neat administrative strokes, nor in the adoption of one set of teaching methods to the exclusion of another. Improvement will come about only from a thorough understanding of the many complexities, and from action on a broad front.

The language of the report reads like that of a critical but supportive friend – professionals speaking to fellow professionals in an attempt to urge and persuade, rather than to command:

> If there is one general summarising conclusion we offer it is that there is nothing to equal in importance the quality and achievement of the individual teacher, to whom most of our suggestions are addressed. All our recommendations are designed to support and strengthen the teachers in the schools, for it is with them that improvements in standards of reading and language assuredly lie.
>
> (DES 1975: 513)

Compare the language of the Bullock Committee with this document which emanated from the same government department twenty-three years later:

> Literacy is at the heart of the drive to raise standards in schools. Shortly after taking office, the new government set a challenging national target for literacy – in 2002, 80% of 11-year-olds are expected to reach Level 4 or above in the Key Stage 2 English tests. It had set up a Literacy Task Force whilst in Opposition, whose final report was published in

summer 1997. This report set out a National Literacy Strategy designed to raise standards of literacy in primary schools in England.

(DfEE 1998: 2)

The differences in tone and emphasis are striking. Where Bullock has 'complexities', 'suggestions', 'recommendations' for 'support' and 'improvements', the *National Literacy Strategy Framework for Teaching* has a 'Task Force' committed to setting 'a challenging national target' in the 'drive to raise standards'.

The change in language noted here represents a significant shift in the English curriculum from the established, Romantic consensus of *cultural heritage* and *personal growth* to an emphasis upon what Brian Cox described as an *adult needs* paradigm which 'focuses on communication outside the school'. The *adult needs* view, Cox continues:

> emphasises the responsibility of English teachers to prepare children for the language demands of adult life, including the workplace, in a fast-changing world. Children need to learn to deal with the day-to-day demands of spoken language and of print; they also need to be able to write clearly, appropriately and effectively . . .
>
> (Cox 1991: 21)

When Cox wrote these words, he imagined that this particular perspective would represent one of five equally important strands woven through the statutory National Curriculum for English; but over the past two decades the emphasis has shifted so much in favour of the *adults needs* view that now even bodies whose function is to champion the cause of creativity and the arts in education feel obliged to borrow the language of the workplace in order to argue their case. Here, for example, are the opening sentences to the first two paragraphs from Chapter One of *All Our Futures*, the report of the National Advisory Committee on Creative and Cultural Education:

> Countries throughout the world are re-organising their education systems. Like us, they are engulfed in rapid economic and social change. One of the most basic expectations of general education is that it will enable young people to get a job when they leave school.
>
> (NACCCE 2001: 18)

This shift in curriculum emphasis from *cultural heritage* and *personal growth* to *adult needs* has major implications for English teachers committed to the Romantic agenda. Within that *adult needs* paradigm, their role is now recast, not as missionaries of culture anymore but – to develop the images implicit in the extract from the *National Literacy*

Strategy Framework for Teaching quoted above – as front-line troops of a 'task force' or as factory workers ordered to meet 'targets' set by their employers. Consequently, the decision to become an English teacher today demands an unprecedented obedience to the dictates of the state. To those for whom Leavis' injunction to 'discriminate and resist' forms the inspirational core of the Romantic teaching agenda, this is a difficult commitment to make. It requires not only a willingness to transmit the forms of cultural reproduction approved by the dominant forces in society (with all that implies for the notions of identity and inclusiveness explored in the previous chapter) but also to accept state approved definitions of what were once dearly held Romantic pedagogical principles and aesthetic concepts.

'Creativity' is one of these. Current governmental rhetoric attempts to link this most elusive and fundamental of Romantic ideas with hard-headed notions of standards, targets and accountability so that the latter 'sneak in', as it were, under the protective 'cloak' of the former. The following extract from the then Secretary of State for Education's introduction to the *Key Stage 3 National Literacy Strategy Framework for Teaching* provides a good example of this:

> Language lies at the heart of the drive to raise standards in secondary schools. It is the key to developing in young people the capacity to express themselves with confidence, to think logically, creatively and imaginatively and to developing a deep understanding of literature and the wider culture.
>
> (DfEE 2001: 5)

That the head of a government agency now called the Department for Education *and Skills* [my italics] might make such a connection between 'standards' and 'creativity' is understandable. That the following statement, similar in intention, should come from the Secretary of State for Culture, Media and Sport seems a little more surprising:

> The arts, business and society all interact, all derive support and enlightenment and life from each other. Creativity in its widest sense is at the heart of much of what we in this country are good at. *It is the foundation of a new generation of high-tech, high-skills industries. Ideas are the building blocks of innovation and innovation builds industries.*
>
> (NACCCE 2001: 19, my italics)

This quotation takes us to the heart of the pedagogical argument. The champions of the Romantic curriculum described in the previous chapter would have contested the assumption that 'business' – as Chris Smith[1] so innocuously puts it here – might sustain the arts. Arnold, Lawrence, Leavis and their fellows were deeply concerned by the impact of mass industrialisation and its attendant consumerism upon both the human spirit and upon the organic communities and natural environments which nurture it. Lawrence, for example, had experienced at first hand the bitter social consequences of what *All Our Futures* describes, somewhat euphemistically, as: 'the incessant need for businesses to develop new products and services and to adapt management styles and systems of operation to keep pace with rapidly changing market conditions' (NACCCE 2001: 19).

In a largely autobiographical extract from his novel *Women in Love* which still manages to create resonances for anyone who lived through the industrial unrest of the early 1980s, Lawrence describes the impact upon his father's mining community of one such early attempt to accommodate 'rapidly changing market conditions'. Rationalisation of the long-established 'butty system' alienates the miners from their labour and destroys both their sense of autonomy and community.

It might seem far-fetched to suggest a connection between the example of unfettered capitalism from the early years of the previous century described by Lawrence here and the contemporary English classroom. The underlying principle, however, remains true. To enrol as an English teacher today is to put oneself at the service of a state for whom the Romantic principles of individual growth into community through the shared experiences of the creative imagination are subordinated to, and placed in the service of, the economic imperatives of the global market-place. The reality of what this means for teachers and pupils becomes only too apparent when the *adult needs* agenda is taken into the English classroom. The Key Stage 3 Sample Standard Assessment Test for 2003 provides a particularly bizarre example of what can happen when the forces of literature and creativity are harnessed in the service of 'business'. The following extract is a question on *Macbeth* taken from Section A of the sample *Shakespeare Paper*.

This examination question which – had it been the 'real' thing rather than a sample would have played a significant part in determining the educational destinies of the majority of fourteen-year-olds attending the state schools in England[2] – represents a considerable loss of faith in the value of literature. The pupils are invited here, not to engage with the power and complexity of Shakespeare's language and thought but, rather, to demonstrate how adept they are at 'shifting product'. There is no sound pedagogical reason why the subject should even be *Macbeth* at all: had the object touted for sale been a video about road safety or personal hygiene, the assessment purposes would have been served just as well. The examination question does not encourage pupils to develop either the 'discrimination' or the 'power to understand what we hear and read' which, to the critic I. A. Richards, represented the goals of critical engagement (Richards 1929: 3). Rather than evaluating the quality of Shakespeare's

Section A – Writing

You should spend about 30 minutes on this section.

People are always looking for new ways to present Shakespeare's plays.

Watch this space!

You work for The Living Shakespeare Company, which is producing a video of *Macbeth* in modern dress. You receive the following memo:

MEMO

To: The Publicity Department
From: Sam Parker

The *Macbeth* video is nearly ready – now we need to persuade schools to buy it. Can you write a publicity booklet for teachers, outlining:

➤   what's on the video;
➤   why it will appeal to young people;
➤   what the educational benefits are.

By Friday?
Thanks,
Sam

Write the text for the publicity booklet.

20 marks including 4 marks for spelling
(QCA 2003: 3)

work, the pupils' task is to sell the video – irrespective of any intrinsic worth it might possess.

This raises a number of pedagogical and ethical challenges for teachers committed to the Romantic agenda. If they are to do the state's behest in this instance – and the consequences of disobedience, in an age of examination league tables and market forces, could be far-reaching in terms of job security – they must shift the focus of their attention away from an engagement with the literary text and concentrate instead on drilling their pupils in the procedures to be followed when constructing – like so many factory workers on an assembly line – the various components of a persuasive publicity brochure. The purpose of such assembly work is, itself, morally questionable. Teachers might well ask themselves if they really came into the profession in order to help pupils acquire the 'glib and oily arts' of salesmanship – no matter how valued those 'arts' might be in the market-places of a world whose economic status quo ensures that 2.7 billion people are obliged to survive on less than two dollars a day.[3] 'Whatever became', such teachers might wonder, 'of the old war-cry, "discriminate and resist"'?

When the utilitarian attack upon the Romantic agenda is mounted from the political right in the heavy-handed manner described here, it seems relatively easy to identify the nature of the challenge and to propose a counter argument – while at the same time indulging in the smug feeling that, by doing so, one has somehow retained the moral and pedagogical high ground. Far more disconcerting are the challenges voiced by theorists operating at a very different end of the political spectrum from James Callaghan or Sheila Lawlor. Stevens will explore these further in Chapter 6; but it is pertinent here to focus upon criticisms of the Romantic enterprise which have been mounted by highly respected English specialists. Gunther Kress, for example, might well argue in support of the SAT question described above; but rather than taking an economic line, he would make the case in terms of democracy and empowerment. Kress' response to the hallowed Romantic concept of 'creativity' is just as utilitarian as that of Chris Smith quoted earlier; but the fact that he is speaking here for all those disaffected young people who, like my pupil Alan, are chafing under the burden of the Romantic literacy curriculum, lends his words particular moral and political authority. Kress asks:

> How many school-leavers will be called on to become 'creative' users of language? How many will be called on to become creative users of the genres which are most highly valued in the school, the 'poetic' or literary genres?[4]

The alternative curriculum Kress proposed over a decade ago could be a blueprint for the National Literacy Strategy:

> One might reset the aims of language education more modestly, more realistically and more usefully to give students skills in the use and manipulation of language, to give them a fuller understanding of the manifold meanings of language and of the genres with which they will come into contact.
>
> (Kress 1994: 126)

The ethical challenge raised by Kress' critique of the Romantic literacy curriculum is more complex and difficult to refute than that posed by the SAT question discussed earlier. Why should not Alan, and the many pupils who seem to share his views, decide for themselves what literacy experiences they need? It is, after all, their one chance of education that is at stake here. What right has the Romantic English teacher to impose the study of Tennyson's *Mariana* upon someone who wants to acquire the language skills needed to function effectively at work on the building-site or at leisure with his friends?

I was forced to confront this dilemma in one of its starkest forms recently when I was shown a piece of writing produced for GCSE coursework. The author is a fifteen-year-old boy called Nasrullah. English is not his first language. He had recently moved with his family from Malaysia to the North of England and been assigned to a mainstream English class in a comprehensive school. This is the opening of his piece.[5]

Fifteen September, six fourty seven o'clock. I wake up from the sleep. It is still dark. I look around me. My brother is still not awake from the sleep. I jump from the bed and go down to the dining room.

On my way to the dining room, I heard the phone ringing. i quickly run down and answer the phone.

'Hello, who's talking?'

'It's me, grand ma!'

I know she wants to have a chat with my mum so I quickly wake her up. Both of them keep talking until the clock show seven.

The weather outside is windy. I look at my mum. A seconds later after she put down the phone, she asked me to wake everyone up. She also asked me to settle my disabled brother. I wake everyone up and go back down stairs.

As I arrived, i go sit next to my brother and turn him around. I could not believe what is happening. Blood has come out through his nose and mouth and his body is very cold. I quickly shout out loud calling my mum and dad to go down stairs.

By that time I knew what was happening but i did not say a word about that. My dad quickly tooked him to the kitchen, wash his face which has got blood come out and tried to get him breathing by doing mouth to mouth. My brother went to tell the neighbour to give us a ride to the hospital. No luck, they've gone to work. My mum went to called an ambulance and she even tried to get another neighbour that live not far from here.

The piece goes on to describe most movingly the family's response to the young boy's death and the preparations for the transport of his body back to Malaysia for burial. This is the concluding paragraph:

> We arrived to Malaysia. My grands parents fetched us. The time was about half past four in the evening. It took about up to seven o'clock to get the body's out. Then we went to our villages called [name removed]. That night we did a prayer for him and at nine thrity we interred him. Before that I did touch him for the last time ever in my life. We could not believe that we've noticed that his face looked like an infant which was just born and he even looked like he was smiling. May be to thanks to us. This was the night that I will not forget all my life. When ever i'm reminded of him, i always cried by myself. I looked at the past when i was about eight years old when i tell him a funny story, sing for him and when ever i feel so sad, i always talk to him and tell him my feeling to him.

This is writing of very high quality. Nasrullah has succeeded in describing the pain and grief of death with an intense, heart-breaking honesty. That the writing never collapses into mawkishness is a tribute to the author's remarkably sophisticated control of his chosen medium. Take the first paragraph as an example. In a piece concerned with mortality, it is fitting that the opening should consist of two terse adverbial phrases of time. The fact that they read like camera instructions establishes at once a sense of detachment, of looking in at something from the outside, which buttresses the writing, as it were, so that it is able to support the sequences of emotional intensity which follow. The contrast between the descriptions of the narrator and of his brother is masterly: the active verbs used to depict the former – 'I wake', 'I look around', 'I jump from the bed and go down' – seem to emphasise the contrasting stillness of the dead brother and, on a second reading, to charge such seemingly innocuous statements as 'My brother is still not awake from the sleep' with a tragic resonance.

This piece of writing appears to offer a powerful vindication of the *personal growth* model of English. Here, surely, is a young man using language to bring 'the meaning of experience within the jurisdiction of form' (Heaney 1980: 47). Further, by commemorating in such arresting prose the death of his brother, Nasrullah seems to reach out magnificently towards that goal to which the poet William Wordsworth aspired:

> . . . and I would give,
> While yet we may, as far as words can give,
> A substance and a life to what I feel:
> I would enshrine the spirit of the past
> For future restoration.
>
> (*The Prelude*, Book XI, ll. 339–343)

And finally, by bringing this piece of writing into the public space of the classroom, Nasrullah offers us, his audience, another example of Heaney's 'befitting emblems of adversity',[6] through the medium of which we as a community can share connections between our personal and collective experiences of death and the experiences of the young Malaysian described here – thus opening up another of what David Holbrook described as those vital 'gateways' between individual human beings and the cultures within which they must live their lives.

How is the Romantic teacher to respond to a text like this? Holbrook's 'gateway' metaphor is particularly apt because it evokes images of movement across boundaries – from innocence to experience, perhaps, as Stevens, drawing analogies with the writings of William Blake, put it earlier. In a classroom committed to the *cultural heritage* and *personal growth* models of English, the teacher would hope to act as a guide – or, to use an image which gestures more clearly towards the Romantic idea of English teaching as a priestly vocation – a mediator to assist Nasrullah's passage through the 'gateway'. In this capacity the teacher might – to use again the quote from Holbrook cited in the previous chapter – hope to make links between the 'civilization' which is 'growing' within him and 'the inheritance of civilization on the shelves of libraries and in the English tongue itself'.

Nasrullah, himself, did not see things like this, however. He had no wish to explore further with teacher or classmates the experiences described in the account of his brother's death. Other spaces in his world – his home, for example, or his mosque – provided sites which he considered more appropriate than the English classroom for the contemplation of such deeply personal matters. For him, Holbrook's 'gateway' led in another direction. He simply wanted his teacher to correct the grammatical and syntactical errors in his writing so that he could produce a more effective piece of work and gain a better GCSE grade. He wanted to know, for example, why 'I did touch him for the last time ever in my life' is not deemed to be as acceptable a form of written Standard English as 'I touched him for the last time ever in my life'. It is in encounters such as this that the reality of Kress' suggestion that we should 'reset the aims of language education more modestly, more realistically' begins to bite.

'We can never', Paulo Freire wrote, 'have an educational activity which is a neutral one ... And if education cannot be neutral, it is for domestication, domination or liberation' (in Lister 1973). Reflecting upon these words within the context of the current debate about Citizenship education, Ian Davies identifies a fundamental tension between 'duties' and 'rights' which he summarises in the following question: 'What are students expected to learn: to do what they should do, or to claim what is rightly theirs?' (Davies *et al.* 2002: 115).

We can no longer assume – as we might have done, perhaps, thirty or even forty years ago – that all parties concerned with the enterprise of education share an understanding of what these concepts mean. For a Romantic English teacher to honour Nasrullah's request by narrowing the creative and moral potential of their shared encounter with the text so that it focuses upon the correction of those heartbreaking errors of tense in the narrative, seems tantamount to acquiescence in a pedagogy of, at best, 'domestication' and, at worst, 'domination'. Yet, for Nasrullah, the rigorous correction of inaccurate written English by an expert offered a pathway to that 'liberation' which he believed that the possession of effective literacy skills would bring him. Nor can the sense of binary opposition implicit in Davies' question, quoted above, be taken for granted anymore. What the Romantic English teacher feels that Nasrullah 'should do' with this text is different, not only from what the student claims as his 'right', but also from what government ministers and proponents of genre-based literacy feel English practitioners 'should do' with the very subject itself.

Where do English teachers committed to a Romantic agenda go from here? Are they to abandon their role as 'preacher', 'missionary', 'mediator', 'facilitator' – or whatever term best describes the act of helping growing human beings negotiate their way from innocence to experience – in favour of the transmission of an authoritarian pedagogy focused upon the 'transactional'[7] linguistic exchanges (Britton 1972) of the 'real' working world beyond the school gates?

To take such an approach is to enter dangerous territory. Somewhat ironically, perhaps, it is Gunther Kress himself who identifies the problem:

> Effective teaching of genres can make the individual into an efficiently intuitive, and unreflecting, user of the genre. The genre and its meanings will come to dominate the individual just when the individual feels that he has come to a command of the genre, and this is so whether he be scientist, technical writer, bureaucrat or short-story writer. *The genre will construct the world for its proficient user.*
>
> (Kress 1994: 126, my italics)

The danger is that, rather than creating some kind of Brunerian scaffold which enables pupils to work with increasing confidence within a particular linguistic form, the genre-analysis curriculum could become a means of constraining and containing thought and initiative – an initiation, as Bourdieu might put it, into culturally approved ways of knowing, thinking and feeling. In their understandable concern to teach those genre skills which Kress advocates, teachers may become so involved with the details of the 'scaffold' that they simply take the genre form and its conventions as given – immutable and unassailable. By doing this, we run the risk of instilling in our pupils: 'an obedience to form . . . without any correlative challenge to our discussion of the socially constructed values represented by any given genre' (Myhill 1999: 72).

Here, for example, is Robert Jeffcoate describing how he would teach a form of transactional writing such as the essay: 'I have always supplemented the use of models . . . with advice on possible frameworks . . . and on matters of organisation and style – opening sentences and conclusions, main points and illustrations, paragraphing and subordination' (Jeffcoate 1992: 135).

A pupil might master all of these techniques and write an essay (or a publicity brochure for a *Macbeth* video) which achieves top marks in an examination – without ever asking such fundamental, ideologically charged questions as: 'Why is this particular genre privileged in this way?' 'Who does or does not have access to this genre and why?' 'How does this genre construct the world for its proficient user?' 'What alternative forms of communication might serve equally or even more effectively in place of this one?'

Concern with teaching the structures of genre can create a spurious sense of empowerment, in the same way that an emphasis upon 'consumers' rights' appears to champion the claims of individual citizens while actually conniving at their disempowerment by positioning them within a particular, materialistic power structure. Sitting in a National Literacy Strategy classroom recently, I noticed a 'writing-frame' poster which, in the manner advocated above by Jeffcoate, attempted to define the techniques of persuasive language in terms that a young secondary school audience might understand. The opening lines read:

I would like to persuade you that . . .

There are several points I want to make to support my point of view . . .

I tried to fill in the gaps of the writing frame with a number of possible answers: 'brand of soap powder', 'type of car', assertions about smoking, school uniform or capital punishment. As I did so, it struck me that I could not recall ever reading an effective persuasive text which had been written in that way. As Peter Medway explains: 'In such argument much may be at stake in an attempt to convince or persuade, so that what matters is not presenting the better case but getting the other person to change: anything else is failure' (Medway 1989: 27).

Persuasive texts use a subtle range of rhetorical strategies to achieve their desired effect. They cajole, flatter, frighten, wheedle, joke, look for sympathy, exaggerate – and so on. Above all, they disguise themselves as something else: 'I would like to persuade you that our company's car is better than any of our competitors' models' is unlikely to make the kind of advertising copy which would be snapped up by a motoring corporation.

Commenting upon Mikhail Bakhtin's pioneering critical readings of literary forms, Simon Dentith draws particular attention to the Russian theorist's observations about the way in which the novel, for example, exploits a whole range of genres in order to achieve its effects:

> The novel permits the incorporation of various genres, both artistic (inserted short stories, lyrical songs, poems, dramatic scenes, etc.) and extra-artistic (everyday, rhetorical, scholarly, religious genres and others). In principle, any genre could be included in the construction of the novel, and in fact it is difficult to find any genres that have not at some point been incorporated into a novel by someone.
>
> (Dentith 1995: 215)

What is true of the novel is true of all kinds of so-called 'non-fictional' texts. This is not earth-shattering news. As Ronald Carter observes: 'Teachers regularly identify texts which do not conform to any single generic structure. They are the result of mixed genres.' He cites a number of examples including:

> arguments which make use of narrative structures, narratives which have reporting or exposition structures embedded within them, and reports which are simultaneously impersonal and personal in form: that is, they are reports which also contain personal accounts of events and specific, person-based recommendations.
>
> (Carter 1995: 56–57)

Consider this opening line, for example:

> The Po valley became the renowned region it is today, because of the vision of a great Piedmontese statesman – Camillo Benso di Cavour.

This quotation provides a vivid example of that blurring of generic boundaries described by Carter above. Where might it come from? a short story? a history book? a biography? a travel guide? Perhaps reproducing the whole text will provide a clue to its provenance:

> The Po valley became the renowned region it is today, because of the vision of a great Piedmontese statesman – Camillo Benso di Cavour. In

1855 he supervised the construction of thousands of miles of canals, thus
irrigating one of the most fertile plains in Europe with water from the Alps.
Using the same systems, Italian farmers, selected by [name of company
omitted], continue to produce rice with the same unique characteristics to
provide you with a creamy and velvety wonderful risotto.

This text is, in fact, the blurb printed on the side of a supermarket rice
packet; but one would have to read well into the final sentence before
feeling confident enough to suggest its true identity. It is carefully crafted
and complex enough to bear the kind of critical investigation traditionally
associated with the study of literature. One could make comparisons, for
example, between the way the Metaphysical poet John Donne uses verbal
conceits to compare his 'mistress' with 'America'[8] and the way this text
establishes an equally startling connection between a nineteenth-century
Italian statesman, a twenty-first-century supermarket shopper and the
humble rice grain. The text is rich, too, in carefully structured visual images
which draw the reader's eye gradually inwards from the vast geographical
spaces of the 'Po valley', 'Europe' and 'the Alps' to the physical particularity represented by a plate of 'creamy and velvety' risotto. The language
of the text is carefully chosen to achieve a particular rhetorical effect. In
the opening sentence, for example, the present is linked to an epic past
by a sequence of verbs and adverbs ('became', 'is', 'today'); the sense of
causality suggested by the connective 'because' signals a belief in the power
of heroic individuals to alter the course of history; a cluster of positive
adjectives ('renowned', 'great') and high-minded nouns ('vision', 'statesman'), all serve to weave the story of the risotto – as made by this particular
manufacturer – into the grand narrative tapestry of Italian history.

Each of the six questions asked of Geoffrey Hill's poem *September Song*
at the end of the previous chapter could be addressed to this text, too, with
equally fruitful consequences. To ask 'who speaks this text?' for example
is to invite an exploration not only of ideas concerning authorship and
personal voice but also of the power structures which underpin the creation
and dissemination of this kind of material. The contextual and historical
study which one might bring to a poem by Donne can also shed powerful
light on this text. Readers might wonder, for example, why no mention is
made of the fact that Cavour died of malaria contracted, apparently, in a
rice field – nor of the migrant female labourers who made such a significant contribution to the history of Italian rice production.

If the boundaries between 'literary' and 'non-literary' texts are so
blurred, then the suggestion that the study of the latter is somehow more
'real' and 'relevant' than the study of the former becomes open to question.
Moreover, as the brief analysis of the advertising blurb above suggests, one

could argue that it is precisely those procedures of rigorous and attentive textual scrutiny which Richards and Leavis brought to the study of literature that have enabled us to deconstruct, and thus gain some sense of control over, this supposedly non-fictional text. To accede to my GCSE pupil Alan's implicit request for a utilitarian curriculum based on some kind of drilling in 'non-fictional' writing frames – whether they be job applications or instructions in how to fill in a tax return – would be to impose upon him the kind of 'instrumentalist' or 'skills-banking' literacy (Freire and Macedo 1987) which cause Caliban, in Shakespeare's great play about education, *The Tempest*, to issue that famous cry of defiance against those who would use the forces of literacy to enslave others:

> You taught me language; and my profit on't
> Is, I know how to curse. The red plague rid you
> For learning me your language!
> > (*The Tempest,* I. ii. 365–367)

A truly empowering literacy curriculum would – to borrow and re-direct Kress' observation – teach its students how to 'construct' the genre rather than be 'constructed' by it. In order to achieve this, one must have the ability to scrutinise genre which seek to control us from the outside, even as we are obliged to operate within them. For Jerome Bruner, this capacity to look with fresh eyes – to break what Stevens, citing Blake again, has described as the 'mind forg'd manacles' – is a fundamental requisite of true learning:

> There is compelling evidence that so long as the environment conforms to the expected patterns within reasonable limits, alerting mechanisms in the brain are quietened. But once expectancy is violated, once the world ceases strikingly to correspond to our models of it . . . then all the alarms go off and we are at full alertness.
> > (Bruner 1971: 5)

Several years ago, I was invited to contribute to a book designed to explore key educational concepts from the perspective of different academic disciplines (Davies *et al.* 2002). Keen to demonstrate that literature had a valuable contribution to make to the debate, I took as my starting-point a fascinating novel published in 1992 by the author Peter Dickinson. Entitled *A Bone from a Dry Sea*, the book, which is set in prehistoric Africa, explores as one of its concerns a moment of conceptual breakthrough which has a revolutionary impact upon the evolutionary progress of the ancestors of *Homo sapiens*.

I believe that what Dickinson has to say about the creative process is so germane to this section of the current chapter that I want to call upon him again here. The moment of breakthrough in his novel comes when the protagonist, a hominid whom Dickinson calls Li, makes an inspirational and unprecedented connection between two seemingly mundane images common to her daily world: a spider's web and a pool of fish. By forging this connection, Li comes to the understanding that she could create out of gourd fibre a fishing net which would enable her tribe to catch and eat shrimps whenever they felt hungry and thus free them from their ancient dependency upon the tides and the weather for survival.

Li achieves her conceptual breakthrough because she 'violates expectancy' by looking at the familiar – the web and the pool – in a radically different way. Fundamental to her creative act is the ability to link two totally disparate images, synthesise the information she receives from them and make a third, completely new, image of her own.

In my previous commentary upon this creative moment, I wrote:

> What crucially distinguishes Li from the spider is her capacity to internalise the insect's behaviour and to reproduce it in symbolic form. The spider can do no more than weave a physical web. Li can imitate its actions physically – by weaving together gourd-fibres, for example. More than this, she also possesses the uniquely human ability to 'weave an intellectual web' – patiently to spin threads of connection between the seemingly disconnected and disparate images stored in her memory.
>
> (McGuinn 2002: 40)

The model of the creative process offered by Bruner and Dickinson is endorsed by the authors of *All Our Futures*. Compare Dickinson's description of Li's moment of conceptual breakthrough with this account, cited in the report, of a similar experience recorded by the Nobel Prize-winning Physicist, Richard Feynmann:

> I decided I was only going to do things for the fun of it and only that afternoon as I was taking lunch some kid threw up a plate in the cafeteria. There was a blue medallion on the plate – the Cornell sign. As the plate came down it wobbled. It seemed to me that the blue thing went round faster than the wobble and I wondered what the relationship was between the two – I was just playing; no importance at all. So I played around with the equations of motion of rotating things and I found out that if the wobble is small the blue thing goes round twice as fast as the wobble. I tried to figure out why that was, just for the fun of it, and this led me to the similar problems in the spin of an

electron and that led me back into quantum electrodynamics which is
the problem I'd been working on.

(NACCCE 2001: 29)

Feynmann's emphasis here upon 'fun' and 'play' is highly significant. In
A Bone from a Dry Sea, Dickinson also makes it clear that Li's moment
of conceptual breakthrough comes, not when she is experiencing an
adrenalin-rush of 'fight or flight' anxiety but, rather, when, feeling well-fed
and secure, she has time to observe, concentrate and speculate. The Ancient
Greeks understood this. It is no coincidence that their word for 'school' was
based on their word for 'leisure' – by which they meant that freedom from
what Abraham Maslow described as fundamental, 'physiological' needs
(Maslow 1954) which enables the mind to focus upon intellectual, aesthetic
and spiritual endeavours. It is interesting, too, in this context to note that
the Ancient Greek for 'play' and 'education' are also connected. Ever since
Freidrich Wilhelm Froebel established his first 'kindergarten' for 'the
psychological training of little children by means of play and occupations'
(White 1907: 13) in 1840, the vital links between creativity, learning and
play – 'the only work worth doing', as Caldwell Cook described the latter
(in Hornbrook 1989: 7) – have become increasingly recognised by educational thinkers (see, for example, Bruner *et al.* 1976).

In a seminal essay entitled *Play and its Role in the Mental Development
of the Child*, Lev Vygotsky argued that play exercises an 'enormous' influence on child development (Vygotsky 1976: 544). It could help to socialise
young children and to enhance their sense of morality by inducting them
in the practices of collective, rule-based enterprises such as games, where
concepts such as turn-taking might encourage the individual to understand
that he or she is not the only person in the world who possesses needs,
desires or feelings. More fundamentally important even than this, however,
was Vygotsky's identification of an intimate link between play and the
child's perception of reality itself:

> in play activity, thought is separated from objects, and action arises
> from ideas rather than things. It is through play, in other words, that
> the child learns to inhabit the world of the imagination and therefore
> of the mind; and by doing so, takes the first steps towards intellectual
> and emotional independence: the child sees one thing but acts differ-
> ently in relation to what he sees. Thus, a situation is reached in which
> the child begins to act independently of what he sees ... Action in a
> situation which is not seen but only conceived on an imagined level and
> in an imaginary situation teaches the child to guide his behaviour not
> only by immediate perception of objects or by the situation immedi-
> ately affecting him, but also by the meaning of this situation.
>
> (Vygotsky 1976: 545)

If we look again at the moments of conceptual breakthrough described earlier by Peter Dickinson and Richard Feynmann, we can see how Vygotsky's ideas have informed our understanding of the creative process. 'Why a child plays', Vygotsky argued, 'must always be interpreted as the imaginary illusory realisation of unrealisable desires' (Vygotsky 1976: 539). Both Li and Feynmann have an urge to, literally, think the unthinkable – whether that thought be about the principles of quantum electrodynamics or the design of the world's first fishing net. Drawing upon Vygotskian ideas, Jerome Bruner argued that 'symbolic representation' – the 'capacity to let one thing stand for another' – is the 'psychological factor which transforms human learning' (in Baumann *et al.* 1997: 72). The supreme medium of symbolic representation is language; and it is figurative language, above all, which enables us not only to store and combine complex ideas in our minds but also to communicate them to others. For Feynmann, it is the image of the 'blue medallion on the plate – the Cornell sign' which acts as the catalyst to his thinking; for me, in this sentence, it is the metaphor 'catalyst'; for Li, the link between spider's web and fishing net is triggered by a simile: 'Then a flick of movement caught her eye, speed followed by stillness, like a minnow in a pool' (Dickinson 1992: 26).

In a particularly telling phrase, Vygotsky made another claim for the value of play, one which is particularly relevant to the purposes of this book. By playing, he wrote: 'the child is liberated from situational constraints through his activity in an imaginary situation' (Vygotsky 1976: 544).

Feynmann and Li achieve their moments of creativity because the act of play releases them so that they can embark on an exhilarating, free-flowing journey through the realms of thought and imagination where, liberated from the constraints of the physical world, all connections become possible. We see this same power at work in great poetry – when John Keats, for example (in that poem which brought such trouble to the young Tony Harrison in the previous chapter) attempts to escape 'heart ache' and 'numbness' by riding on 'the viewless wings of Poesy'.[9]

And so we come back to literature. In the previous chapter, I described how, in the 1980s, Peter Medway had contested its perceived domination of the English curriculum, arguing instead that young people in school should have more opportunities to use what he described as 'perlocutionary' language capable of effecting real actions in the world. In some ways, the National Literacy Strategy, with its emphasis upon so-called 'non-fictional' genres, represents a laudable attempt to address the claims voiced by Medway and by the two GCSE pupils to whom I have referred in this chapter. This apparent move towards empowerment, however, has actually done nothing to enhance the status afforded to young people's writing in schools. No matter how many supposed letters of complaint, magazine advertisements or persuasive essays for or against fox hunting they write, they are no nearer effecting real change than they ever were.

The extract from the sample SAT paper quoted earlier provides a good example of this. Despite all the efforts of the author(s) to make the question look and read like an authentic memorandum, it still remains an examination question pretending – or playing, even – at being something else. The 'publicity brochure' which the pupils are meant to write in response will be read by examiners, not potential customers; rather than bring in money, it will be used to sort out academic 'sheep' from academic 'goats'. If we were to do what Medway asks us to do and really afford status to pupils' spoken and written language, we would have to undertake a profound, revolutionary reappraisal of our attitude towards the nature of schooling and of the power relationship between young and old.

Until this happens, the least we can do is to reject the sham play-which-pretends-it-isn't-play described above and reassert the importance of literature, that language form whose very purpose *is* play – in the full, Vygotskian sense of the word. Drama teachers, whose pedagogy is particularly sympathetic to the ideals of the Romantic English teacher, understand this well. The Brazilian practitioner, Augusto Boal, has seized particularly upon Vygotsky's ideas. One can hear echoes of that essay on play cited earlier in the definition of 'theatre' which Boal offers here:

> in its most archaic sense, theatre is the capacity possessed by human beings – and not by animals – to observe themselves in action. Humans are capable of seeing themselves in the act of seeing, of thinking their emotions, of being moved by their thoughts. They can see themselves here and imagine themselves there; they can see themselves today and imagine themselves tomorrow.
>
> (Boal 1992: xxvi)

Boal has harnessed the creative potential of play to most radical and – to borrow Peter Medway's term – 'perlocutionary' effect through the medium of Forum Theatre. Here, Vygotskyian concepts of 'activity in an imagined situation' are played out, literally, when the 'spect-actor' strives to be 'liberated from situational constraints' not only by acting out the reality of what Boal calls his or her 'oppression', but also – by simultaneously reflecting upon those actions within a fictional space – exploring the possibility of transformational change in the 'real' world. The fictional space in which drama takes place – whether it be located in a Brazilian *favella* or an inner-city comprehensive school classroom – becomes a site of real cultural power because it allows the imagination and the discourses which sustain it to run free. A disempowered adolescent can become a queen whose commands have to be obeyed; a fairy story like *Little Red Riding Hood* can be transformed into a bridging metaphor which helps young children negotiate some kind of understanding about their fear of bullying.

The study of literature can do these things too, particularly when it draws upon the strategies used by drama practitioners. Here is a brief extract from a tape-recording of a GCSE pupil (not Alan this time, unfortunately!) responding in the character of Shakespeare's Ariel during a drama-based 'hot-seating' exercise designed to explore *The Tempest*. The questioner has just asked 'Ariel' why s/he remains so faithful to Prospero:

Ariel:	I'd quite like to walk out but I know that I owe it to him . . .
Questioner:	But you don't really have the guts . . .
Ariel:	No, not really . . . because he's still got the power . . . I find it a bit unfair that Prospero uses the fact he saved me against me. If I do anything wrong he'll put me back in the tree.[10]

Here again is a manifestation of Stevens' move from innocence to experience, of Holbrook's passage through the gateway from the world of the self to the wider culture in which that self must make its way. The young pupils involved in this exchange are not only accessing Cox's *cultural heritage* model of English by engaging with the language and ideas of Shakespeare; they are also using that literary text as they might use a drama space: to explore potentially painful and complex ideas – about obedience, fidelity, obligation and the nature of power – which can impinge so strongly upon the lives of adolescents. The young girl speaking from the perspective of Ariel here is striving to create that 'live circuit . . . between reader and text', between *personal growth* and *cultural heritage*, which Louise Rosenblatt regarded as fundamental if the exploration of literature is ever really to provide 'a *living-through*, not simply *knowledge* about' (Rosenblatt 1970: 25, 38).

Literature 'plays' in another way, however. It plays with metaphor and simile, with pun and alliteration, with ellipsis and ambiguity, with subtextual meanings, with silences as well as sounds. Take just this very brief quotation from Shakespeare, for example, and consider how the metaphors flow along the line like quicksilver, evoking complex ideas about time, retribution, dishonesty, concealment and exposure with masterful concision:

Time shall unfold what plighted cunning hides
(Shakespeare, *King Lear,*
1, i, ll. 282–283)

Literature is also playful in a Vygotskian sense in that it can challenge our perceptions of reality. In his instructive and entertaining analysis of Ernest Hemingway's short story *The End of Something*, Nick Peim demonstrates how framing structures which we take for granted in our daily lives are contested by the medium of fiction:

> The most apparently obvious categories are, at times, the ones that can seem most bizarre. Take, for instance, the idea of place. Simple questions can make this category seem quite problematical, if we grant the reading the kind of status given to conventional reading practices. This may begin with: Where is Horton's Bay? [the place where the story takes place] Is it in the story? Or is the story in it? Or just near it? What kind of place is it? Is it a fictional place with only fictional identity granted to it by this story? – in which case the only existence it has is determined by what's given in and by the story. Or is it a real place that has been put into a fictional context?
>
> (Peim 1993: 18)

The principles of pedagogy which lie closest to the heart of the Romantic English teacher are not luxuries to be abandoned at the behest of economic and utilitarian imperatives. They are fundamental to our humanity as moral, spiritual and social beings. They provide the well-springs which sustain the creativity without which no progress – cultural or economic – is possible. The ways of seeing and knowing which they encourage help us to negotiate our uniquely individual place within a culture – and they teach us how to be critically literate so that we can read, as Paulo Freire put it, both the 'word' and the 'world' (Freire and Macedo 1987). If we educators have failed to convince pupils like Alan of this, the fault does not lie with Tennyson.

5 'Taking the mind to other things'

Romanticism and the new technologies

> A tool is a particular thing, but it is more than a particular thing, since it is a thing in which a connection, a sequential bond of nature is embodied. It possesses an objective relation as its own defining property. Its perception as well as its actual use takes the mind to other things.
>
> (Dewey 1981)

Teachers committed to a Romantic vision of English teaching could be forgiven for viewing the Information and Communication Technology (ICT) revolution with misgivings. So many of the cultural and pedagogical practices which sustain it seem incompatible with that sense of Romantic vision with which Stevens concludes the book in Chapter 6. One could argue, for example, that ICT represents a particularly extreme and potent manifestation of the 'technological mindset' which has so heavily influenced the epistemologies of Western thought for the past two centuries (Bowers 1982: 530); or that it is an insidiously powerful tool by means of which cultural, economic and political elites maintain their privileges (Ellul 1964; Feenberg 1991); or that its arrival marks the ultimate triumph of some kind of Bakhtinian nightmare in which one 'normative' language dominates the globe.

For Sally Tweddle, speculating almost a decade ago about the possible impact of ICT upon the English curriculum, these concerns seemed real enough:

> [Information Technology][1] carries a threat of producing a new generation of haves and have-nots in a society which increasingly values knowledge as the key to wealth and power; in a global economy which depends upon technological literacy; in a multimedia culture for which linear print literacies are inadequate.
>
> (Tweddle 1995: 4)

Reliable data about ICT use around the world are notoriously difficult to collect; but, given this proviso, some recent figures (Ash 2000) seem to bear out Tweddle's concerns. As in so many other areas – whether it be health, education or economics – so in terms of access to ICT: a fault-line has opened up between the industrialised nations and the so-called 'Third World'. According to Ash, the top ten countries with the most computers at the turn of the millennium belonged to the former category, with America, of course, leading the way (164,100,000). The next closest was Japan with 49,900,000; while China trailed in at eight with a mere 15,900,000. The figures for Internet use tell the same story: again, the top two places were shared between America (41 per cent of the population) and – lagging well behind – Japan (14 per cent of the population). China, again, came in at eight with 6,308,000 users. English proved to be the most common language used by individuals accessing the Internet (91,969,000) with Japanese a poor second again (9,000,000). Major world languages like Mandarin and Russian could only manage 5,600,000 and 1,300,000 respectively (Ash 2000: 209).

The drive towards linguistic conformity can be observed on a micro as well as a macro level. ICT has spawned its own discursive practices and taxonomies, many of which are controlled by a handful of global corporations. What might have seemed like a new, exciting textual space has already been colonised. Familiar words – 'program', 'drive', 'worm', 'spam' (!) – have taken on new meanings with which to confuse (and exclude?) the uninitiated; particular physical and cognitive procedures have to be learned and followed through in order to access software packages and Internet resources; self-access learning materials take individual pupils, working in isolation with a computer rather than a human teacher, through rigidly programmed exercises which allow scant opportunity for dialogue or interaction. The writing process, itself, can be subjected to an ostensibly benign 'policing' by cartoon-style icons which offer templates for business letters or memoranda, or by grammar and spell-checking devices which urge the adoption of a particular syntactical form or punctuation convention – and which are thrown into confusion when invited to 'proof read' an extract from a poem or piece of unconventional prose. All this seems a long way from the 'open', 'intercultural' classroom which Stevens describes in Chapter 6.

In the important article cited earlier, Tweddle attempted to create a conceptual model robust enough to accommodate the challenges posed by the ICT revolution to our conventional understanding of the ways in which texts are constructed, mediated and received. One category suggested by her model carries a particular resonance for this book: the 'gatekeeper'. Tweddle envisaged that, in the context of 'electronic communications systems', the gate-keeping role would be played by 'individual and/or institutional arbiters of what will be published in the form of conference moderators or service-provider censors' (Tweddle 1995: 9). The implications are more widespread and more profound, however, than this account suggests. It could be argued that, in terms of access to knowledge and the authority it bestows, we are witnessing today in the Western world a shift in the balance of power more dramatic than anything seen since the time before the invention of printing when book learning was concentrated within monasteries and controlled and mediated by monks. We might flatter ourselves that we are 'computer literate' – by which we mean that we can utilise all the tools on a word-processing program, prepare a multi-media slide presentation or even author our own web-pages; but we are far less likely to know how to repair a computer when it 'crashes', or how to create a sophisticated software package, or who the ultimate controllers of the Internet might be. It is with the people who can do these things that the real power resides.

Viewed from this perspective, our vaunted 'computer literacy' can seem like something very different – its 'instrumentalist' or 'skill banking' counterpart (Macedo 1994: xv) which, Paulo Freire argued, the powerful bestow upon the weak in order the better to service the latter's oppression. In its bleakest form, ICT has the potential to give a post-Fordist twist to Marx's account of the way in which workers can be alienated from their labour and from the means of production. Thus, someone working at a supermarket check-out point, for example, might experience maximum responsibility with a minimum of autonomy: the sophisticated computerised till they 'control' is capable of processing complex amounts of information about individual customers' shopping habits and the work-patterns of the till operators themselves – but all the operator has to know is how to be pleasant to the customers while pressing a series of buttons. Colin Lankshear argues that this kind of application of ICT is part of a deliberate deskilling process:

> if only the relatively small proportion of knowledge workers necessary for modern economies . . . actually *need* high order literacies; if, beyond 'demands for basic numeracy and the ability to read', routine production and in-person service work call primarily 'for reliability, loyalty, the capacity to take direction and . . . a pleasant demeanour', why *wouldn't* we expect 'literacies' to mean for most students 'basic competencies', and 'technological literacy' to mean 'keyboarding skills'?
> (Lankshear *et al.* 1997: 5)

The vision of work depicted here would have been abhorrent but also sadly familiar to the twentieth-century proponents of a Romantic English curriculum and to the Victorian thinkers who helped shape their ideas. For Thomas Carlyle, writing in 1843, it would have represented an inevitable consequence of 'the ascendancy of industrialism and utilitarianism' which, sixty years after the advent of the Industrial Revolution, had already 'fragmented the "brotherhood of man" into millions of atoms, each person a faceless, nameless nullity' (Carlyle 1915: xi). The alternative proposed by writers like D. H. Lawrence or educators like F. R. Leavis and his disciples, G. H. Bantock and David Holbrook, sought to recapture the union of body and spirit and the William Morris-inspired delight in creative labour, described so lovingly by George Bourne in this portrayal of a village wheel-wright written some eighty years after Carlyle's *Past and Present*:

> Truly it was a liberal education to work under Cook's guidance. I never could get axe or plane or chisel sharp enough to satisfy him; but I never doubted then or since that his tiresome fastidiousness over tools and handiwork sprang from a knowledge as valid as any artist's. He knew, not by theory, but delicately, in his eyes and fingers.

Bourne continues:

> in them [Cook and his fellow craftsmen] was stored all the local lore of what a good wheelwright's work should be like. The century-old tradition was still vigorous in them. They knew each customer and his needs; understood his carters and his horses and the nature of his land; and finally took a pride in providing exactly what was wanted in every case.
>
> (Bourne 1963: 33)

Reading this Romantic account of idealised labour, one is struck particularly by Bourne's depiction of the relationship between the wheelwright, his work and his tools. The American educational thinker John Dewey wrote:

> A tool is a particular thing, but it is more than a particular thing, since it is a thing in which a connection, a sequential bond of nature is embodied. It possesses an objective relation as its own defining property. Its perception as well as its actual use takes the mind to other things.
>
> (Dewey 1981: 101)

The wheelwright's tools serve to 'take [his] mind to other things' by affirming his sense of himself as an expert. Moreover, by creating a 'connection' with his customers and with the 'century-old tradition' from which he learned his craft, they affirm, too, his sense of identity within a community, a culture and a history. 'The point is', as Blacker and McKie write in their response to the quote from Dewey,[2] 'that the materiality of the [tool] recedes from conscious awareness in favor of a dynamic world of meaningful involvements, ever expanding and contracting' (Blacker and McKie 2003: 235).

It is difficult to imagine a computerised tool like a supermarket check-out till affirming its operative's sense of autonomy and identity in the same life-enhancing manner. Teachers who possess the supposed mastery of 'computer literacy' skills described earlier, might feel that their relationship to ICT as a 'tool' is much more positive than this. However, ICT also poses a threat to their autonomy and professionalism – albeit one that is ultimately more subtle than the overt form portrayed above.

The most obvious manifestation of this threat lies in the fact that ICT could well render the whole concept of school as a physical institutional presence obsolete. If I can pay for one-to-one, on-line tuition from Ms X, the world's finest Maths teacher who happens to live in Australia, what is the incentive to sit in a shabby, ill-equipped classroom where I have to share the attentions of the less than inspirational Mr Y with thirty other pupils, several of whom are intent only on disrupting his lesson? The proliferation of e-learning initiatives, of on-line teaching and mentoring programmes and of websites dedicated to the provision of tutoring advice and resource material for subject specialisms, suggests that this process is already well under way.

The more complex form of the threat to teacher autonomy and professionalism, however, lies in something which seems, at first sight, to be a strength rather than a source of potential vulnerability. Research into initiatives designed to increase teacher competence in the use of ICT (Goodwyn *et al.* 1997; Harrison *et al.* 1998) suggests that teachers are, generally, keen to engage with the new technologies. Commenting on his work with English teachers in 1997, Goodwyn remarks:

> Just over half the teachers were clearly now 'optimists' and these were teachers of all kinds of ages and degrees of experience. They felt that ICT was empowering and stimulating, providing genuinely new forms of communication and means of gaining information and access to texts of all kinds, that it broadens the whole concept of literacy, giving children and adults masses of opportunity to be active learners and meaning-makers.

Goodwyn adds: 'However, they had no illusions about magic solutions; *they identified many problems associated with access to equipment, training for teachers and the oversimplistic view of computers held by some who saw them as replacing teachers*' (Goodwyn 2000: 8, my italics).

This is where the problem lies. It is the same point that was made in earlier chapters when we explored Gunther Kress' concern about genre's capacity to 'construct the world for its proficient user' or considered the pedagogical implications of teaching the Key Stage 3 sample SAT writing question on Shakespeare. The danger is – and Stevens returns to this point in a wider context in Chapter 6 – that teachers take the ideological

structures upon which ICT is predicated as given and thus fall into the political trap identified by the Frankfurt School of radical critics (Habermas
1970; Horkheimer and Adorno 1991) wherein, preoccupied with perfecting
the 'means' – 'How can I get access to technical support?' 'Where can I find
in-service training?' 'Give me the title of an effective spelling package' – one
never has time to stand back and question the 'ends'. And thus, again,
teachers run the risk of becoming technicians rather than autonomous
professionals. As Blacker and McKie so tellingly put it:

> Elites not only use technology as a club, but also to conceal that there
> is any clubbing going on at all. It provides a perfect weapon, effective
> yet invisible. And the more value-neutral we regard it, the more
> invisible it becomes.
>
> (Blacker and McKie 2003: 241)

In his important recent summary of developments in English teaching
and ICT, Richard Andrews demonstrates his awareness of this potential
danger by skilfully attempting to balance references to 'means' and 'ends'
in his vision of future developments. Identifying 'five principles to guide the
effective integration of the new technologies into classroom-based literacy
education and to guide curriculum activity more generally', Andrews writes:

> In terms of implications for English teachers at primary and secondary
> levels, these [five principles] distil into a need for continuing pro-
> fessional development in the application of the new technologies
> to the subject – not only, for instance, as part of government-funded
> schemes for the training of teachers in ICT, but also as part of a longer-
> term understanding of the need for teachers to keep abreast of new
> developments and new conceptions of their subject; complementarity
> in the sense of understanding how ICTs affect conventional practice,
> how they may be integrated with conventional writing practices
> and how they may change the landscapes of practice in the classroom,
> especially in relation to home learning; workability in terms of sensible
> solutions to learning needs in a school, rather than technology-driven
> purchasing that creates imbalances in the learning community of the
> school; equity in the sense of making sure that English teachers and
> students get equal access to computer equipment and software with
> other curriculum areas.

It is significant to note, however, that, despite the skilful accommodation
of both 'means' and 'ends' accomplished here, Andrews concludes this
particular policy statement on the future of ICT and English with a sentence
which locates him clearly within the *adult needs* camp inhabited by
Gunther Kress and Peter Medway:

Finally, the emphasis on trajectories implies that English work in schools will have in mind the kind of discourses used in the real world, not only to create simulations of these in the classroom but also to exchange communication with the world beyond school and to equip students to operate confidently with the discourses of that world (or those worlds).

(Andrews 2001: 140–141)

If English teachers accept the ideologies and epistemologies underpinning ICT as givens which cannot be contested, if they cast themselves in the role of technicians bound to the service of a technology which is, itself, committed to an *adult needs* educational agenda, the consequences will be profound. Tools have the capacity to shape, as well as be shaped by, the user. Citing the philosopher Wittgenstein, Fleming and Stevens observe that 'words acquire their meaning by use rather than by any simple relationship with reality' (Fleming and Stevens 1998: 69).

Unquestioning acceptance of the supposed 'givens' of ICT could force Romantic English teachers to surrender some of their most important concepts so that they are appropriated and redefined by the dominant discursive practices of technology. 'Knowledge' is one of these. In his famous opening to *Language and Learning*, James Britton draws an analogy between the map-making with which he and his brother charted and recorded their youthful explorations of the physical landscape around the family home and his personal mental exploration of the metaphorical landscape of ideas, experiences and feelings in which, as a growing young man, he was attempting to negotiate a cultural space for himself:

The map was a record of our wanderings, and each time we returned we added to it or corrected it. It was, though a crude one, a representation of the area; we valued it as a cumulative record of our activities there. Furthermore, looking forward instead of back, the map set forth our *expectations* concerning this area as we approached it afresh each time. By means of it we might hope to move around more purposefully, more intelligently.

(Britton 1972: 11)

The sustained metaphor which Britton uses here to describe the process by which human beings acquire knowledge of themselves and their world is one which strikes a responsive chord with Romantic English teachers. Not only does it reaffirm the importance of Jerome Bruner's 'symbolic representation' as the prime medium by which the transformations essential to learning are effected; but also – through its suggestions of hesitant, exploratory movement, of tentative efforts to chart a way forward by making reference to past discoveries, of slow-dawning enlightenment and of coming upon the familiar with fresh eyes – it articulates that Romantic sense of learning as *personal growth:* a gradual, patient, guided movement from innocence to experience.

This learning agenda is very different from the one which focuses the attention of ICT practitioners. When Sally Tweddle attempted to predict the future impact of the new technologies, she identified the main challenge as follows:

> Firstly, IT [*sic*] is producing an information-rich society in which many more people have access to vastly greater quantities of information than they have ever had before. How they gain access and how they are equipped to handle that information are key issues.
>
> (Tweddle 1995: 4)

This same concern with the challenge of the 'information-rich society' also exercised another important thinker about ICT, Richard Lanham, who made it a central strand of his argument that the rhetorical arts should be positioned once more at the core of the curriculum:

> What seems to be the universal experience is not that we are short of information, but that we're drowning in it. It's been compared to trying to drink from a fire hose. What's in short supply is the attention, the human attention which takes information or data and makes useful information out of it. I conclude therefore that really when we say we're in an information economy, what we're really talking about, we're talking about naming it by the scarce commodity – that we're in an attention economy ... You might define rhetoric, instead of the classical definition of the art of persuasion, as the economics of attention. It tells you how to persuade somebody to attend to one body of argument rather than another.
>
> (Lanham 1996: 42)

The contrast between Britton's image of the map and Lanham's image of the gushing hose is a stark one. In Lanham's vision, the world of discourse becomes a cacophonous market-place whose occupants are a crowd of hawkers, each trying to shout down the other in order to sell their wares. Potential 'customers' – and the term is carefully chosen – have to think quickly if they are to make the right purchase; and when the time comes for them to sell something in their turn, they have to shout faster, louder and more authoritatively than any of their competitors. Compare that description to the poet William Butler Yeats' portrayal of another craftsman at work – not a wheelwright this time, but the Renaissance painter Michelangelo – in his magnificent poem, *Long-Legged Fly*. Here, the act of creativity is evoked, not through noise, but through the image of an artist's brush moving in almost utter silence across the ceiling of the Sistine Chapel. In the 'communicative maelstrom' (Andrews 2001: 133) of the contemporary world, where time and attention are at a premium and silence is a rare commodity indeed, what place remains for the intense, rapt, patient concentration so essential to the creativity of Bourne's wheelwright or Yeats' painter? In such a world, the possession of 'knowledge' – and I have in mind here Britton's observation that 'Every encounter with the actual is an experimental committal of all I have learned from experience' (Britton 1972: 15) – runs the risk of being confused with the ability to access and manipulate 'information'; in the same way that 'training' in computer skills may be mistaken for that ability to comprehend and engage with the epistemologies and deep ideological structures of ICT which 'education' would bestow.

The quotation from James Britton cited above reminds us that 'time' is another important concept contested by ICT and the Romantic vision of English education. The rhetoric associated with the former is concerned primarily with looking forward. Writings about English and ICT – even those which include a review of past initiatives and developments – usually conclude with phrases such as: 'The plan is', 'As I write I can look forward', 'mapping the future' (Tweddle 1995: 11); 'we have not even begun', 'we . . . enter a new age' (Goodwyn 2000: 132); 'far-reaching implications for the future of communication', 'things will change', 'it is possible to imagine that in a few years' time' (Andrews 2001: 142, 143).

To these expressions of anticipation, Romantic English teachers might well respond by quoting the lines from William Wordsworth cited in an earlier chapter: 'I would enshrine the spirit of the past/For future restoration'. Engagement with the past through the medium of the *cultural heritage* model of literature matters, they might argue, because – as Seamus Heaney said of poetry – it is concerned with 'divination . . . revelation of the self to the self . . . restoration of the culture to itself' (Heaney 1980: 41). The past matters, too, in the sense suggested by the brief quotation from Britton cited earlier: it is only because we have 'learned from experience', that we are able to make our 'experimental committal' to 'the actual'.

This sense of the past as a personal and cultural repository from which individuals can draw the resources they need in order to comprehend and assimilate new experiences is connected to Bourne and Yeats' depiction of craftsmanship at work – and even to Britton's image of hesitant exploration – by shared metaphors of stillness, concentration and contemplation. The images associated with ICT, however, are concerned with speed and fluidity (Lanham 1993). ICT is, literally, a fluid medium because the pixels from which its electronic texts are composed are, themselves, fluid. The day before writing this, when working on a report in my office at York, I needed a contribution from a colleague who was lecturing in Japan. I emailed him with a request for the information, he emailed it back and I pasted it into the document. No matter how familiar we become with anecdotes such as this, it is difficult not to wonder at the revolutionary, almost miraculous, way in which ICT has transformed our understanding of time, speed and communication. How long would the exchange I have described above have taken one hundred, or even fifty, years ago?

ICT is also fluid in a more profound, metaphorical and ethical sense. The move from the stability of print to the fluidity of the pixel means that 'the long reign of black-and-white textual truth has ended' (Boltor 1991: 2). As my anecdote suggested, texts which are not fixed in print upon a page and bound between the covers of a book can be manipulated and passed instantaneously around the world to an audience of indefinite size – and the members of this audience can, in turn, subject the original document to intense revision and re-organisation before passing it back to its source. There are major implications here for the *cultural heritage* model of literature. If we can do these things to the memorandum which I sent speeding through cyberspace to Japan, we can do them also to canonical literary texts. And if the 'printed book . . . seems destined to move to the margin of our literate culture' (Lanham 1993: x), then so, too, might the concept of 'the author' – as Sally Tweddle foresaw when, in her conceptual model of 'a text framework', she replaced this term with the word 'Originator': 'No major document produced today, whether from government or commerce, is likely to have been written by a single hand. People will use computers and communications systems to write with others or to take their ideas and reshape them' (Tweddle 1995: 7).

Once a text is downloaded and saved electronically, it comes under the structural control of the person who has 'captured' it. Whole chapters of a novel, for example, might be re-arranged so that the author's original, linear narrative sequence is disrupted. One could write pastiches of the chosen piece and insert them into the text. One could add interpolations selected from the works of other writers different in time, culture and style or even from a totally different genre. And so on. The point is that these interventions move us a long way from Romantic ideas about the integrity of the literary text or of the creative process as the mysterious, intimate and private 'somnambulist encounter' described by Seamus Heaney. Taken to its extreme, this technological world in which any text can be infiltrated, subverted, inverted, disguised or restructured at the caprice of its electronic 'keeper' reveals disconcerting similarities to what Nicholas Tate, former Chief Executive of the Qualifications and Curriculum Authority for England, described as: 'that pervasive relativistic view of the world . . . which sees everything as some kind of a construct: artificial, ephemeral, the result of choices and structures that come and go and in which no authority resides' (Tate 1999: 13).

If ICT takes us down this road, we will have arrived at a very bleak place indeed:

if one adopts, in a cavalier and single-minded fashion, the view that everything is discourse or text or fiction, the realia are trivialized. Real people who really died in the gas chambers at Auschwitz or Treblinka become so much discourse.

(Megill 1985: 345)

How, then, should English teachers committed to Romantic ideals respond to the challenge of ICT? Readers could be forgiven for assuming, from the tone of this chapter so far, that they are being urged to adopt some extreme Luddite position regarding the new technologies. To do so would be pedagogically and morally irresponsible. Refusal to join ideological battle would leave the field in the possession of those 'gatekeepers' whose intention – to use the language of Bourdieu and Jürgen Habermas – is to accumulate the 'high status' knowledge of ICT as another form of 'cultural capital' which they might put to the service of 'instrumental rationality' – an educational agenda very different from anything espoused by Romantic English teachers.

Habermas (1970) proposed a countervailing, radical educational curriculum which – through its emphasis upon collaborative, active learning, the empowerment of the individual voice, the development of critical literacy skills, the celebration of diversity and an awareness of the role of the citizen – might foster and sustain a truly democratic and egalitarian culture strong enough to contest the global impulses towards hegemony, standardisation and instrumentality described by Stevens in Chapter 6. These latter forces have been portrayed consistently throughout this book as inimical to Romantic educational ideals; and in Habermas' proposals – not least his belief in the importance of aesthetic education – English teachers sympathetic to those ideals might find an enabling pedagogy which can help them to engage with the enormous challenge (and potential) of ICT on terms of their own choosing.

The way forward is to consider the technology through that lens of playful creativity shared, as described in an earlier chapter, by the protagonist of Peter Dickinson's novel *A Bone from a Dry Sea* and by the Nobel Prize-winning Physicist, Richard Feynmann. The following extracts provide a vivid example of what I mean. Here, Rob Stannard brings a sensibility grounded in the *cultural heritage* and *personal growth* traditions imaginatively to bear, through the medium of metaphor, upon the creative potential of the Internet. Stannard's knowledge of canonical texts (Swift's *Gulliver's Travels*, Dante's *Divine Comedy*, the poetry of Tennyson and the myths of Ancient Greece) furnishes him with a series of 'gateways' – in the sense of the word which both Stevens and I have explored throughout the book – through which to make powerful connections between his personal world and the new world of cyberspace:

There are echoes of explorations of other spaces in earlier times, to other ages of navigation and expansion, and of technologies that opened up hidden worlds in this iconography [of the Internet]. There are references to the voyages of Columbus and Magellan and of imaginary voyages like that undertaken by Gulliver ... The names of search engines include 'Magellan', the sixteenth-century Portuguese navigator ... 'Yahoo', one of a race of brutish creatures resembling men met by Gulliver on his travels ... The Web has been likened to a labyrinth which echoes the story of Theseus who needed Ariadne's thread to find his way out of one and of Dante's *Divine Comedy* in which the poet is in need of a guide through the phantasmagoric worlds through which he travels and which are themselves analogues of the universe. There is, perhaps, also a resonance with the story of the Lady of Shallott, who wove a tapestry of a world reflected in a mirror.

(Stannard 1997:16–17)

Through the playful use of metaphor, again, Stannard is able to make startling and evocative connections between the world of human communication and the world of science:

New technologies foster a new collective. The analogy here is that of the rhizome. A rhizome is an underground rootlike stem of a plant, the roots and shoots of which are both separate and collective. The kind of global interconnectedness fostered by the Internet is like the rhizomatic mode of connectivity.

(Stannard 1997: 19)

Each of these metaphorical connections – whether it be the links between *Gulliver's Travels* and the nomenclature of search engines or *The Lady of Shallott* and the web-like structures of the Internet – opens up wonderful opportunities for exploration and I urge all Romantic English teachers to read the whole of Stannard's article. The image which resonates most powerfully for me is the one described below. Stannard continues: 'The final analogy is of the "book". Our word for text derives from the Latin *textus* meaning something woven. We derive our word "textile" from the same source. And there is a woveness to all texts' (Stannard 1997: 17).

This image stimulated my imagination so that I started to make my own connections between what Stannard writes here about the etymology of 'text', the web-like structures of the Internet and something Richard Andrews said about 'the hyped world of electronic communication' with its 'window-framed looks on to entire landscapes of print' (Andrews 1997: 1). My own attempt to imitate the playfulness of Richard Feynmann and Rob Stannard was to try to link 'text' to 'frame' in a way that might accommodate Habermas' radical teaching agenda. The negative connotations of framing – its capacity to focus our gaze in set, preordained patterns – have already been explored earlier in the chapter. But could a computer not also be a weaving-frame – a loom upon which language is spun in new, imaginative designs? This metaphor has a particular appeal because it gestures, not to the bleak image of the computerised supermarket check-out, but towards the sense of craftsmanship – of delight in labour – implicit in George Bourne's Romantic depiction of his village wheelwright or William Butler Yeats' description of Michelangelo at work on the Sistine Chapel; and by doing so, it attempts to bring the new technology within the imaginative compass of that vision.

The act of viewing the computer through the medium of this metaphor allows us to focus upon its capacity for liberation rather than constriction. Nowhere is this more powerfully apparent than in its potential to transform the very process of writing itself. ICT can do this physically by removing the orthographical constraints which come into play when pen or pencil meet paper; and it does so on an intellectual and affective level by giving the writer permission, as it were, to make mistakes and to try again. To discard a manuscript written in longhand is to squander a considerable investment of time and effort; but a document composed electronically can be copied and stored in as many versions as the author wishes:

> Different versions of a text can be created, saved and displayed – either on the screen or in hard copy form – for comparison and further composition. Texts can be reviewed at different levels: their spelling, grammar and textual structure can be scanned.

However, as Andrews continues:

> The great value of all this is not so much the technical wizardry, but the opportunity it gives us to play with language shapes, to reframe them according to different needs, to subvert propriety as well as to observe it.
>
> (Andrews 1997: 2)

The writing of this chapter, itself, provides an illustration of Andrews' point. If I had been composing with pen and paper, I would have worked from a sequence of three physical texts spread before me on a desk: the notes from my reading, the sketched outline of the chapter and the chapter itself. Thinking about the computer as a weaving-loom, however, encouraged me to configure these three texts differently. I imagined them as three separate strands of cloth placed side by side upon the loom and then established a practical application for the metaphor by placing each text into an individual window on the computer, so that I was able to move simultaneously from one to the other as indicated in the table below:

Notes from my reading	Ideas for the chapter	Final draft
	Wittgenstein. Language contested. We start to see through the eyes of the technology. Some of our most cherished terms are taken over (as 'creativity' and 'cultural heritage' were hijacked). This could be for example 'knowledge' which for us has intimate connotations of how the self negotiates a place within the culture (use Britton's analogy of the map here). Danger that ICT replaces 'knowledge' with 'information retrieval skills'.	In such a world, the possession of 'knowledge' – and I have in mind here Britton's observation that 'Every encounter with the actual is an experimental committal of all I have learned from experience' (Britton 1972: 15) – runs the risk of being confused with the ability to access and manipulate 'information'; in the same way that 'training' in computer skills may be mistaken for that ability to comprehend and engage with the epistemologies and deep ideological structures of ICT which 'education' would bestow.
Page 151: 'The application of this criterion to all of our games necessarily entails a certain level of terror, whether soft or hard: be operational (that is, consummerable) or disappear.' Lyotard.		
Lyotard's critique of 'performativity' – we only value what can be sold as a commodity, rather than valuing knowledge for its own sake – COULD BE APPLIED TO MY SECTION ON 'KNOWLEDGE' AND 'INFORMATION'.		

Working with pen and paper, my movement from initial reading to planning to final draft would have followed a much more linear, chronological sequence. By allowing me to view the three stages of the compositional process at the same time, however, the computer frame enabled me to break away from that linear pattern and to move at will – 'backwards and forwards in time', as it were – between final draft and initial thoughts. Thus, when I came to include the quotation from James Britton shown above in the 'final draft' column, I was prompted to look again at the preliminary notes I had made in the first column and add here, for future reference, the comments indicated above in block capitals.

This reference to the font used for composition is also important; for one particularly valuable aspect of the computer's 'technical wizardry' is its ability to give a writer access to a wide range of marking devices. Thus, here, I was able to use block capitals to distinguish secondary comments on my reading and also to colour-code my writing, choosing red for titles and drafts, blue for the commentary, green for planning and black for the final version. This important feature of reading and writing on the computer screen gestures towards Howard Gardner's theory of multiple intelligences (Gardner 1993) but also, as Richard Lanham has pointed out, takes us back to a much older way of reading and writing the world:

> The rhetorical figures ... were often called the colours of rhetoric. Figured discourse, which is to say, patterned, ornamental discourse, was often described in terms of colour imagery. What people were trying to do was introduce that part of the visual cortex which processes colour into a spoken or a black and white textual field.
>
> (Lanham 1996: 41)

Given enough time and resources, there is no reason why this chapter – or the whole book – might not have exploited the 'wizardry' to its fullest extent in the manner of Marvin Minsky's 'expanded book' *The Society of Mind* described here by Lanham:

> When the title page comes on, first of all it comes on to the accompaniment of music. Then the letters which form the title roll on in three-dimensional blocks and form a pattern. The pattern is in colours. So already you have added a sound signal and colour, which is very important, and a dynamic text ... Then just before the title blocks stop rolling, Marvin Minsky himself peers up over the bottom of the frame of the computer, just like Kilroy on a fence, with half his head and his fingers on top ... As soon as you enter the first chapter you see an audio-visual block with three symbolic faces on it and you can click one and select a discussion, and then the author himself walks on the

stage . . . and then starts to wave his hands around, to gesture and to comment on the arguments in his own book.

(Lanham 1996: 41)

The relatively 'low tech' applications which I employed in the construction of this chapter may not have been as dramatic as the radical challenges to our conventional thinking about writing and reading described here by Lanham; but even they cast new light on the compositional process. The second column of my chart, particularly, proved to be an especially innovatory textual space. What began as a series of brief jottings started to transmute into something more stylised as I added dates to the increasingly dialogic entries:

September 27 2003

Where to next?

- Silas Marner and the loom/Bourne's wheelwright
- Stannard on aesthetic possibilities
- My writing as an example
- Lanham on the book – good challenge to the authoritative text which, we have already decided, needs to go
- Democratises through text-mapping and Brecht
- Jarman's notebooks

Stannard's interesting metaphors to describe looking through the window of the web or back at ourselves through its mirror.

Metaphors of space and movement.

How do I work Habermas into this?

- ✔ Britton's map analogy makes sense because of incremental negotiation with landscape. Ideas of returning and of movement. ICT always looks forward. Heaney. Guidance from Innocence to Experience.

As the notes started to assume the conventions of a journal, so the style in which I wrote began to take more account of the idea that I was writing for myself as an audience. This proved immensely liberating because it meant that the second column became a place where I felt I could say whatever I wanted to say in whatever way I wanted to say it, without worrying about how an outside audience might receive the text. At difficult moments in the writing process, when I had a sense of where to go next but was not clear about how best to articulate it, I was able to 'thought-shower' ideas in the second column – to write my way through the block, as it were – while at the same time cross-referencing the material in the other two columns. When the computer becomes more than a 'glorified typewriter' in this way, one develops some appreciation of that union between thought and action which George Bourne celebrated and which, writing more than twenty years ago about possible classroom applications of the new technology, Seymour Papert identified as the true pedagogical potential of the computer: 'What is most important in this is that through these experiences the children would be serving their apprenticeships as epistemologists, that is to say learning to think articulately about thinking' (Papert 1980: 27).

If we apply a different framing metaphor to the computer, and start to think of it in terms of a theatrical proscenium arch, we open up its potential as a site in which play – particularly dramatic play – can be put to the service of Habermas' radical pedagogical response to 'instrumental rationality'. The links between gaming, imaginative role-play and computers are well-established (Lanham 1993, 1996; Zancanella *et al.* 2000); but detailed analogies, too, can be drawn between the conventions of theatre and the conventions of electronic communication (Laurel 1991; Turkle 1995). What Stannard says here about the dramatic potential of the Internet holds good for many other forms of ICT as well in that they, too, encourage us 'to lose inhibitions and prejudices and to try out alternative identities and virtual personae' (Stannard 1997: 19). Just how powerful that particular experience of play can be is demonstrated in Zancanella *et al.*'s account by a 20-year-old describing his early experiences with a video game:

> It was so immersive to me, so powerful because I became a part of a different world, a world where my participation, my courage, my dedication were vital, crucial to the world's continued existence. A world where I was being evaluated mostly on how hard I was willing to try and how clever I could be.
>
> (in Zancanella *et al.* 2000: 87)

The opportunities for imaginative play which ICT affords must exercise a strong appeal for Romantic English teachers because they are fundamentally concerned with the development of empathy – that profoundly moral purpose which the study of literature shares with the practice of drama. Indeed, Richard Lanham has suggested that the potential for role-play provided by ICT offers a new opportunity to revitalise the personal growth model of English: 'It can be argued that we in fact grow not by continually thinking about ourselves, but in fact by playing other kinds of roles and learning to internalise them from the inside' (Lanham 1996: 91).

The imaginative and moral potential of these playful applications of ICT was brought home to me when I conducted a number of small-scale research projects involving secondary school pupils a few years ago (Babbage and McGuinn 2000; McGuinn 2001). Two groups of under-achieving adolescent boys with very low reading ages – one from a school in inner-city Leeds, the other from a school in High Wycombe – were paired as email reading-partners in the study of George Orwell's novel, *Animal Farm*. The boys were given opportunities to engage in imaginative role-play by communicating through email with 'characters' from the novel. One such task required them to tell the exiled 'Snowball' about what had happened on the farm in his absence. The boys entered into the spirit of the game by willingly suspending their disbelief. Each one began his reply with the words 'Dear Snowball' and each one addressed Snowball as if he were a living presence. One boy actually signed off with the words: 'from your friend.' Some boys entered into the fiction by responding to Snowball's request for information and advice:

> so I think that you should get Napoleon [the new ruler of Animal Farm] worried until he sends his dogs to find you.

Others replied as if they were characters in the novel – even though they had not specifically been asked to do this:

> If we can somehow kill the dogs [Napoleon's body-guards] you can take over the Animal Farm[3]

The boys expressed emotion and a sense of urgency in their emails:

> All of us wish you would come back . . .
>
> Animal Farm is in deep danger . . .

They were eager to report Napoleon's crimes to Snowball, accurately drawing upon events from the novel to do so:

> Boxer [the heroic cart-horse who is the mainstay of the farm] died Napoleon and the pigs sent him to the knacker yard and Napoleon is killing some of the animals and the pigs are keeping the food for themselves.

Some of the boys were able to write sustained, articulate and even impassioned emails from the perspective of unsympathetic characters. In this example, the author is speaking as Mr Jones, the hated previous owner of Animal Farm:

> My dear friends what is this rumour which I have heard around the farm that I don't care for you and I'm an enemy to you. For example I given you a roof over your head's and then in the winter you stay warm. If I didn't give you a roof you would freeze to death. You Boxer do you remember when the stone got in your shoe and who took it out? It was me who took it out and if I didn't put any shoe on your feet imagine in how much pain you would be in. When you are old I'll make sure that you die quick and painlessly by sending you to the Butcher. You cows if I didn't milk you imagine in how much pain you would be in. You sheep if I didn't shear you imagine how hot you would be in the summer.

One unexpected bonus arising from this project was the relationships which the boys from the two geographically distant schools established with each other through the medium of email. We witnessed something which Sally Tweddle had predicted: 'the replacement of traditional teacher and learner roles by new forms of peer tutoring and group work . . . in the new information-rich electronic classroom' (Tweddle 1995: 10). When the boys first started to email each other, they indulged in a great deal of showing-off and assertions of power of the 'your [football] team is rubbish – we'll murder you in the League' variety. As the project developed, however, this tone gave way to something quieter – more vulnerable, even. They started to focus upon Orwell's novel, sharing reports about reading progress:

> where are you up to in animal farm we are up to the beginning of chapter eight

> I have finished my leaflet about Napoleon and I got some pictures from the Internet on the leaflet.

As Tweddle predicted, the boys started, unbidden, to evaluate their own and their email partner's work:

> My best work so far is Mr Jones' speech

> I like your speech in the style of sqealer [one of Napoleon's henchmen]

They started to ask each other – again, unbidden – the kinds of questions traditionally associated with teacher-initiated classroom discussion:

> Who do you think is better to lead Animal Farm, Snowball or Napoleon?

It was as if the relative anonymity and privacy afforded by email allowed these boys, normally so concerned with looking 'cool' in front of their peers, the opportunity to explore language registers, 'rhetorical positions' (as Lanham might put it) and alternative identities to which the 'real' world rarely offered them access. It is difficult to imagine, for example, that the writer of the following text would be prepared to stand up in a classroom and admit to either the behavioural and academic shortcomings or the endorsement of a major canonical writer offered here:

> I could have wrote much more but earlier I was misbehaving, and I was sent out of the I.T. department. So what are you doing at the moment? We are doing Shakespeare, and I really like it. I can't really read some of the difficult words because I am not used to the spellings.

When asked, before the project started, to suggest what its purpose might be, the boys acknowledged that it was designed to bolster their enthusiasm for reading and writing but felt that its ultimate value actually lay elsewhere:

> I think this project is going to be about reading and writing. I will get thoughts of someone and we will be helping each other.

> I think this project will be quite fun. But I think it will be about reading and writing and helping each other. And it helps us make more friends.

> I think it's good. You're starting to get to know each other and you're helping each other with your work.

As their emphasis upon the word 'help' indicates, what the boys valued most about the enterprise was its potential for extending their network of friends. It came as little surprise to us that the participants from both schools insisted that the project should conclude with a face-to-face meeting culminating in a football match.

This capacity to establish a sense of community through shared experience is another potential benefit which ICT can offer teachers committed to a Romantic vision of education. In another small-scale project reported in the same journals mentioned above, two groups of eleven-year-old pupils – one from a fee-paying boarding school and one from an inner-city comprehensive – were invited to share experiences about the transition from primary to secondary education. Although the pupils themselves assumed that their worlds would have little in common, their email exchanges actually revealed striking similarities, as this dialogue extract poignantly suggests:

> I am in red house [the comprehensive school groups pupils pastorally in a 'house' system]. I don't think you have got any houses and I don't think you understand what I am talking about.

> At night it is very scary walking to Red House (the name of our house where all the first years live) because there are a lot of bushes where other years can hide or jump out at you.

And again:

> I have one cat and two rabbits. They are called Rosey and Charley.

> I have 2 ponies called Rupert and Spott and 2 dalmations called Toffee and Fudge.

These small-scale examples of what Stannard describes as a 'rhizomatic mode of connectivity' (Stannard 1997:19) have been replicated on a national and international scale. Voiskounsky (2001) for example, has described how the various Russian populations of the former Soviet Union, dispersed over 'one-sixth of the globe surface' (Voiskounsky 2001: 38) have established a vibrant and culturally productive 'virtual' community via the Internet. In the United Kingdom, too, numerous special-interest groups, ranging from student teachers (Leach 1997) to morris-dancers (!) use the medium of the Internet to sustain and celebrate their cultural identities.

There is one final imaginative connection to be explored through the medium of the computer/theatre metaphor. Just as the radical German dramatist, Bertolt Brecht, used the acting style of *Verfremdungs Effekt* (distancing or making strange) as a tool with which the theatre might probe and expose the ideological structures underpinning the political status quo, so Romantic English teachers can exploit ICT to disclose the ways in which 'authoritative' texts of all kinds seek to position the reader. Using the wide variety of marking devices which the technology places at our disposal, for example, we can 'text map' a piece of writing – by colour-coding its various linguistic features, by commenting upon what we read as we read it, by animating the text so that words and letters move across the screen, or by creating hyper-links with other texts. If transposed from 'print' to 'pixel', for instance, the values implicit in the blurb on the side of the rice packet described in the previous chapter could be brought out into the open – by the creation, say, of a 'hot-link' to websites dedicated to the economics and politics of global rice production or to the history and culture of the female migrant workers whose unacknowledged labour sustained the supposed success trumpeted on the side of the packet. Techniques such as these[4] can provide young people with a powerful, multi-sensory model of resistant reading – one which not only challenges ideological assertions, but also encourages a fundamental reappraisal of 'common-sense' assumptions regarding the linear, chronological nature of the reading act itself (Snyder 1997).

All of these strategies can be placed at the service of Jürgen Habermas' radical pedagogy because they are concerned with active learning, with collaborative enquiry, with the celebration of diversity and with the promotion of 'tolerance for ambiguity and difference' (Zancanella *et al.* 2000: 102). For these reasons, English teachers committed to sustaining the Romantic vision of education in the twenty-first century must harness the potential of ICT to their purposes. This cannot be achieved alone, however, because they lack the scientific knowledge truly to comprehend the deepest workings of the technology. To be truly, playfully, creative, to grapple with the ends rather than merely the means of education, English teachers need to share their vision with colleagues in other subject disciplines and thus, at last, as *All Our Futures* so eloquently argues, heal the age-old division between arts and science.

6 Romantic culture and the intercultural imperative

The unpoetic view of things is that which considers everything to be
dismissed through the perceptions of the senses and the findings of our
understanding; the poetic view is that which goes on for ever interpreting
them and sees in them an inexhaustible fount of images. . . . Thereby everything comes alive to us.

August Wilhelm Schlegel

As we have tried to demonstrate throughout this book, there is no reason
why those stalwarts of the English curriculum, personal imaginative growth
and subjective aesthetic awareness, should be incompatible with social
development and dispassionate critical appraisal. And, by the same token,
there is every reason for creatively connecting a fundamentally Romantic
sense of wonder with an interculturally oriented critical literacy, elicited as
both may be by enterprising and resourceful English teaching. Required
here is a meaningful synthesis, a re-conceptualisation of what English
teaching could mean for the twenty-first century, in terms of both theory
and practice. This is, effectively, the continuing message of the present
book. It is important that the emphasis is on genuine, principled synthesis,
rather than envisaging English as something of an eclectic collection of half-
realised ideas: a bit of personal growth here, and some cultural heritage
there, leavened by adult needs with a sprinkling of critical literacy to
assuage any remaining radical tendencies. As Burgess (Burgess *et al.* 2002:
33) has pointed out, specifically in relation to the teaching of writing in
English classrooms but with far broader implications:

> the right approach is surely synthesis. It is not impossible to conceive
> a practice that attends to the kinds of modelling and to the more
> explicit forms of instruction that are proposed through concentrating
> on text, but does not neglect attention to the writer or to wider cultural
> considerations concerning literacy. . . . It would be a loss to English if
> at the point of seeking to implement new strategies and practices too
> much emphasis were placed on contrast with past practice rather than

on continuity. We should stop presenting work on genre and text as if it were in opposition to the practice hammered out in classrooms where attention was paid first to pupils' learning and to a wider sense of culture, and give space for the development of ideas.

What matters in the end is good classroom practice, combining elements of both established and new ideas on English teaching: effectively re-invigorating and re-orienting the tradition.

In some ways, the secondary school may seem an inappropriate place for any sort of radical movement towards mutually respectful interculturalism. There are at least two very basic threats to any such project and, consequently, a constant struggle to convert them into some kind of opportunity. First and foremost, state schooling is founded unavoidably on compulsory attendance for pupils, and even within this major compulsion there are many minor – sometimes seemingly arbitrary and pointless – limits placed on students' freedom. Furthermore, most schools are, in practice, profoundly authoritarian and even anti-democratic in structure and behavioural modes – hardly the best preparation for full critical participation in a democracy. The second threat is rather more amorphous, and concerns the enclosed, often inward-looking nature of schools, in general terms, as institutions. Rivalries, jealousies and insecurities frequently characterise the social life of students in the school situation, exacerbated no doubt by the anxieties of adolescence and the tremendous surge of libidinous energy that accompanies it. Many adults in my experience, looking back on school days or meeting again in adult life their former school-fellows, feel that some sort of mutual amnesty should be granted on all the petty cruelties practised while in the cauldron of secondary school. In many respects Blake's *Songs of Experience* are uncannily accurate sketches of secondary school life – *The Poison Tree* or *The Sick Rose* are enacted time and time again, with or without teachers' awareness. I mention all this as a warning that idealistic teaching has to be seen in a broader context, which is certainly not entirely favourable. And yet, as the hedge-school teacher portrayed in Friel's *Translations* acknowledges, 'it's all we have'.

With this reality-check firmly in mind, it seems necessary, in effect, to re-position the Romantic outlook away from Rousseau-inspired idealistic individualism (whether or not subsequent interpretations do any real justice to Rousseau's originality of thought and action) and towards the robustly critical and radical socially oriented tradition initially developed by figures like Blake, Thomas Paine, Percy Shelley and, later in the nineteenth century, William Morris. Significantly, we can also include Karl Marx in this venerable tradition, focusing on his emphasis on the dialectical transformation of the damaging dichotomy, so characteristic of capitalism, between the individual and the social, the subjective and the objective:

Though man is a unique individual – and it is just his particularity which makes him an individual, a really *individual* communal being – he is equally the *whole*, the ideal whole, the subjective existence of society as thought and experienced. He exists in reality as the representation and the real mind of social existence, and as the sum of human manifestations of life.

(in Fischer 1973: 23)

In this chapter I intend, particularly, to look at the intercultural dimension of this position, as suggested and briefly defined previously, as a way of reaching the tentative synthesis advocated by Burgess above, and of sensing the particular relevance of this synthesis to the post-modern age.

It is important too, however, to acknowledge the kinds of opposition to the Romantic outlook within education and beyond, and McGuinn has taken a close look at this area in Chapter 4. From the perspective of the educational right, Romanticism may seem like dangerous progressivism, ignoring the realities of schooling in favour of escapist idealism. Hirsch, for example, concentrating on the American context and signalling his disparagement of Romanticism through the title of his paper 'Romancing the Child', maintains that

> the fundamental beliefs of progressivism are impervious to unfavorable data because its philosophical parent, romanticism, is a kind of secular theology that, like all religions, is inherently resistant to data. A religious believer scorns mere 'evidences'.

(Hirsch 2001: 3)

So, by Hirsch's own implication and subsequent exposition, hard evidence, rigorous targets and formal instruction are privileged over any notions of woolly, progressive child-centredness – perhaps not an entirely unfamiliar scenario. From the viewpoint of the radical, materialist left comes a rather different attack, and one that is to be taken seriously. The tone was set some time ago. Hoare (1977: 43), for example, having first praised the Romantic tradition's 'affirmation of humane values against the inhuman priorities imposed by the economy', continued that

> this tradition has failed to transcend its oppositional, escapist character, and has failed to do more than salvage a minority from being broken by the system. It has been burdened by its acceptance of romantic conceptions of the individual personality which have reinforced rather than challenged the prevalent British orthodoxy stemming from Locke, which sees each child as possessing *given* faculties which must be brought out by education.

This is, indeed, strong criticism, and serves to highlight precisely the dangers of the Romantic position. However, Hoare goes on to acknowledge that: 'one of the most crippling failures of the socialist intellectual tradition ... has been its failure to integrate ... the romantic and anarchist "moment" ....'

In the context of a critical reading of Hoare's paper, for 'integrate' it may be more realistic to read 'appropriate'. However, this point notwithstanding, dialectical integration of these two strands of educational thought and action – the radical and the Romantic – is exactly what is demanded twenty-five years on.

More recently, in a purposeful and important article, Medway (2002) has powerfully made the case for a newly coherent philosophical basis for English teaching, focusing on its particularity as an arts subject in the context of enhanced literacy across the entire secondary curriculum:

> Our theory ... needs to give an account of language as art, art as practised through language. Many of the uses of language that English is now expected to develop (reporting, analysis, arguing) can be practised in other subjects. But the distinctive thing about English is its concern with representations of the world and experience, and language used aesthetically.
>
> (2002: 6)

From a radical perspective (and one already elucidated by McGuinn in Chapter 3), Peim has suggested that 'English is significantly under-theorised' (Peim 2003: 33). Maybe, but it seems to me that it is not so much the lack of theory which is damaging, but the lack of a powerfully motivating synthesis of theoretical strands – for both teachers and learners of the subject. And beyond this is the urgent need for a meaningful synthesis of theory and practice: praxis, in effect.

Once again, Marx is helpful here in his critique of simplistic, vulgar materialism:

> the chief defect of all materialism ... is that the object, reality, which we apprehend through our senses, is understood only as the *object* of *contemplation*; but not as *sensuous human activity*, as *practice*; not subjectively. Hence in opposition to materialism the *active* side was developed abstractly by idealism – which of course does not know real sensuous activity as such.
>
> (in Fischer 1973: 152)

'Sensuous activity' seems like an apt description of the English classroom at its most vividly challenging and vibrant, along the lines of the picture we are attempting to construct here. For this kind of sensuous activity to flourish, there must exist a principled openness to intercultural experience. Marx's view of language in this context is equally telling, as expounded by Lefebvre:

> It is not language which generates what people say. Language does not possess this magical power, or possesses it only fitfully and dubiously. What people say derives from praxis . . . arises out of real actions, real struggles in the world. What they actually do, however, enters consciousness only by way of language, by being said.
>
> (1968: 72)

Another radical – and highly influential – educational thinker, John Holt, has contrasted the rigidity of what he calls the 'traditional classroom', characterised by inflexible, authoritarian uniformity of approach, with what he terms 'the open class'.

> The structure of the open class is complicated. It has as many elements as there are teachers *and* children in the classroom. No two of these elements are alike, and their differences make all the difference, since no two children will relate to the class and teacher, or make use of them, in quite the same way. Secondly, the structure is flexible and dynamic. The relationship of each child to the teacher and to the class changes from day to day, and may change enormously in the course of a year. Indeed the nature of the whole class may change. Finally, the structure is organic, internal. It grows out of the needs and abilities of the children and teachers themselves. They create this order . . . When and because they create it, the order works. . . . It does not squelch life. It enhances it.
>
> (Holt 1972: 20)

The strange thing is, all teachers know this – it's what keeps most teachers teaching, and it's what keeps teaching and learning alive. But having the confidence to develop this kind of insight into praxis, often in the face of the destructive instrumental rationality so systematically pervasive – that's another matter. It may well be that in order to gain this sort of confidence, the teacher must consciously, deliberately embrace a measure of insecurity – Keats' idea of 'negative capability' again springs to mind – as part of the learning process. Again, this is realistic, as Segal (1998: 201) points out:

> Although a teacher must plan her lessons, there is much in the actual teaching situation that cannot be planned in advance. These include the ways that students respond to, 'look at' or gaze at the teacher. . . . These contingencies give rise to a sense of unpredictability which may culminate in a subjective sense of uncertainty in the teacher.

Teaching, after all, is not for the faint-hearted, or for the unquestioningly obedient uncivil servant.

Blake, in one of his *Memorable Fancies* from *The Marriage of Heaven and Hell*, wrote that: 'If the doors of perception were cleansed, everything would appear as it is, infinite'. This seems an apt guiding principle for the intercultural project incipient in all of us: an appreciation of the infinite possibilities in all things, and particularly human beings. To return to Blake's tantalising advice, from the epic *Jerusalem*:

> I give you the end of a golden string,
> Only wind it into a ball,
> It will lead you in at Heaven's gate
> Built in Jerusalem's wall

There is a clear signal here of the role of the visionary artist – and of the teacher, visionary or not. This verse, it seems to me, encapsulates the role of the intercultural teacher – even if we're not always sure what sort of culture Heaven, or even Jerusalem, belongs to. Essentially it alludes to the balance – or perhaps tension – between the teacher and the student. The teacher provides the tantalising end of the string, like the hedge-school teacher in Brian Friel's play *Translations*, who, despite a painful awareness of his circumstantial limitations, is intent on providing 'the available words and the available grammar'. The student, if sufficiently inspired and motivated – and it's a significant *if* – winds the ball. It suggests also a balance between teacher involvement in the process of learning and the ability to stand back, to give space. And for this to happen, there is a need for a capacity to 'de-centre' from the teacher – a sense of knowing how it feels to discover anew without undue interference, yet with the security of guidance if and when required. All these are essential features of the intercultural classroom, concerning itself with the microcosmic interculturalities of the classroom population itself as well as the broader implications of global cultural meetings. As Blake had it, 'To see a world in a grain of sand': truth is to be found not in grand statements but in the 'minute particulars' of life. This may be an apt comment on the nature of poetry too, emphasising its synecdochal qualities, and suggesting its centrality as both means and end of intercultural teaching.

By way of contrast to Blake, *All Our Futures: Creativity, Culture and Education* (NACCCE 1999) is committee-written and, as we have seen through McGuinn's analysis, certainly open to criticism. However, as a rare official report on creativity in education it is, nevertheless, valuable. According to this report, focused as it is on the nature of the arts in the English education system, the foremost purpose of cultural education (and by implication, intercultural education too) is to 'enable young people to recognise, explore and understand their own cultural assumptions and values'. The report goes on to elaborate:

> Most young people belong simultaneously to a range of different cultural groups and communities. . . . All young people, particularly during adolescence, are faced with a complex task of constructing a sense of personal identity from what is now an accelerating traffic of images, ideas, pressures and expectations that surround them from home, friends, street culture, the media and from commercial interests of every sort.
>
> (NACCCE 1999: 49)

Arts education, specifically when focused on English teaching in the present context, has a powerful role to play in making sense of this welter of confusing impressions – and not just during adolescence. As well as forging an idea of self-identity, such an education should provide the opportunity to understand, tolerate and empathise with other possible identities, both for oneself (whether teacher or student, for the boundaries inevitably dissolve) and for the other. The experience of reading literature gives us cause to reflect on these areas, holding up a mirror to our own cultural identities in order that this reflection may occur. In a rather more complex way, too, it allows for multiple reflections in so far as each reader, in the collaborative conditions of the creative classroom, brings new meanings and interpretations. It is perhaps, as ever, best to leave it to a poet to say this more succinctly and suggestively: Shelley describing the intercultural power of poetry in his passionately argued *A Defence of Poetry*:

> A poem is the image of life expressed in its eternal truth. . . . the creation of actions according to the unchangeable forms of human nature, as existing in the mind of the creator, which is itself the image of all other minds. . . . [It] is universal, and contains within itself the germ of a relation to whatever motives or actions have place in the possible varieties of human nature. . . . Poetry is a mirror which makes beautiful that which is distorted.

This, then, is the flash of insight, carefully nurtured as it should be through proper teaching, that may give rise to the intercultural perspective. If it does not happen, in some form or another, the most rigorously structured study of the nuances of native and other cultures may be doomed to failure, or, at best, superficiality. Although what we are talking about here is an intensely personal experience, it is also intensely interpersonal – intercultural, in fact. As Imison puts it (in NACCCE 1999: 50):

> If you only understand one culture it is like seeing with one eye only, but if you add the dimension of other cultures, you become binocular and things can be seen in perspective. It allows you to appreciate much more.

And the added appreciation is in terms of appreciation of one's own value – like a precious artefact – as well as simply broadening one's outlook by adding to the number of different cultures one is aware of. Literacy is, itself, a vital ingredient here, in that the meaning of words is culturally determined and developed, in a dialectical fashion. Literacy, in this context, should focus on controversial words and meanings – conceivably *all* words and meanings – in terms of identity and value. Take the expression 'asylum seeker', for example: just how has this couple of words come to express such moral outrage and media-inspired revulsion, when taken in different contexts each word has previously signified something far more positive? Or the word 'refugee', in a similar way: I was observing a particularly unruly lesson in a challenging school recently when an absconding pupil was referred to by his teacher, technically correctly, as a 'refugee' from the lesson. At this the pupil bristled aggressively – for him this was a base insult.

   With thoughts of praxis, as outlined above, very much in mind, it may be instructive to ask again 'what would the intercultural classroom (in the literature-based context already outlined) actually look like?'. The following example centres on the teaching of Craig Raine's poem *A Martian Sends a Postcard Home*. If, in the present context, the appeal of poetry is to engender a sense of wonder in our familiar surroundings through the stretching, exploratory use of language, then this poem performs that role admirably. I have been greatly impressed by the responses of Year 7 (age 11–12) pupils, in a mixed ability class, to a reading of this poem – responses which showed a depth of feeling for the strangeness and wonder of life which I and other adults present in this lesson found quite startling. Raine's poem, of course, belongs to the 'Martian' school, for whom the 'making strange' of the familiar is central. As James Fenton, a fellow 'Martian' poet, has observed of Raine: 'He taught us to become strangers in our familiar world, to release the faculty of perception and allow it to gorge at liberty in the field of experience.' The metaphor brings us vividly back to the wandering/wondering sheep of the Zen koan. Freedom to gorge is all very well, of course, but, at the same time, any act of teaching or learning necessarily suggests a border of sorts, and the tension between the wide pasture and the sought for boundary (opportunity and form, essentially) is potentially a creative one. As Heather McGowan cleverly puns in her novel *Schooling*, 'to write, one only needs a pen. Of course, by pen I mean enclosure' (McGowan 2002: 227).

In senses such as these there may be a helpful echo of Brecht, for whom, 'alienating an event or a character means first of all stripping the event of its self-evident, familiar, obvious quality and creating a sense of astonishment and curiosity about them' (in Brooker 1994: 191).

Brecht's term *Verfremdungs Effect* is appropriate here: a potentially liberating, even celebratory, de-familiarisation. McGuinn has previously, in Chapter 5, demonstrated the helpfulness of this concept in relation to English teaching. Warnock (1976: 197) elaborates usefully on this essentially imaginative process:

> the creative artist, then, constructs an external form which is to be interpreted as signifying something which does not, in the same sense, exist. Both artist and spectator have to detach themselves from the world in order to think of certain objects in the world in a new way, as signifying something else.

From a rather different perspective, we are all indebted to Wittgenstein for showing us something of the inherent strangeness of language as habitually used: what may be termed, in a phrase itself curiously apposite to the project of native language teaching, the poetics of everyday life. The attendant tension between involved engagement and critical distance must, surely, be central to the notion of the intercultural classroom. Like so much else of value, too, this notion is essentially Romantic: Shelley in his *Defence of Poetry* (1821) maintained that poetry, potentially, 'strips the veil of familiarity from the world ... [and] ... purges from our inward sight the film of familiarity ... It compels us to feel that which we perceive, and to imagine that which we know'. This seems as good a starting place as any.

For the teaching of Craig Raine's poem, the lesson comprised several stages:

- The teacher reading the poem aloud, with copies previously distributed to each student.
- Subsequent discussion on the nature of the poem, with an explanation given that the poem deals with eight different everyday objects or experiences seen through the eyes of the 'Martian' visitor to Earth.
- Whole-class guessing as to what precisely these objects/experiences may be. Several are pretty self-explanatory, although couched in unusual terms, such as

  > Mist is when the sky is tired of flight
  > and rests its soft machine on the ground:
  >
  > then the world is dim and bookish
  > like engravings under tissue paper.

Others take more discovery, which is where the fun lies. For example, the telephone:

> In homes, a haunted apparatus sleeps,
> that snores when you pick it up.
>
> If the ghost cries, they carry it
> To their lips and soothe it to sleep
>
> With sounds. And yet, they wake it up
> Deliberately, by tickling with a finger.

And the penultimate object, the lavatory, can cause much amusement – and not a little bemusement before successful guessing of the 'answer'.

- Small groups then discuss, note and report back to the whole class on possible subjects drawn from familiar everyday experience, with a view to eventual poetic expression.
- A further variation here might be to include photographic or artistic representations of 'normal' objects seen from unusual angles, or in a new light (both literally and metaphorically), again with the possibility of awakening from the unseeing contempt so often bred by familiarity. There is in this the opportunity to develop a media-based exploration of images.
- Students then fashion their ideas and observations into 'Martian' poems, using the given convention of the Martian visitor trying to make sense of Earthly objects, customs and ideas. Possibilities include school (especially in the light of the comments I made at the start of this chapter about the nature of secondary schools – an opportunity for real critical insight here), money, items of furniture, and articles of clothing. Illustrations might also be interesting. Volunteers go on to read poems aloud, with the class guessing the subject matter of each poem.

I include some examples of extracts from poems written by students following this scheme of work, to give a fuller flavour of the possibilities:

> It lives on the ceiling
> It never moves
> But when it grows dark
> It gets angry and explodes.
>   Kimberley, age 14

I lie there watching the world
Through a television that's been switched off
I feel so scared
I daren't even cough.

> Laura, age 12

It's a giant snake with many mouths
Which travels very fast
Swallowing all its victims whole
But people wave as their friends get eaten.

> Paul, age 12

It is important in planning and teaching literature-based work that acknowledgement is made of the likely stages of learning. In case this seems rather deterministic and mechanical, ignoring the subtle nuances of classroom relationships, we need, too, to keep a realistic sense that what is *taught* does not necessarily correlate in any predictable way to what may be *learned*. This important rider notwithstanding, it is useful to envisage the stages of learning in terms of:

- the descriptive – the initial reading of the poem, for example;
- the reflective – which may include general or specific textual discussion and questioning;
- the speculative – the kinds of activity arising from textual study, such as pupils writing their own poems, stimulated by, but possibly wandering some way from, the initial reading.

Clearly, the implication of reflection is as some sort of mirroring process; in itself it is not sufficient to provide a sound basis for the speculative, active, creative stage. As well as the *reflective*, then, we need to cater for and stimulate the *illuminative*, whereby the active begins to develop from the passive. In terms of *A Martian Sends a Postcard Home*, the poem suggests it is possible to find in everyday experience exciting scope for observation, description, reflection and illumination, not least through empathetic consideration of the 'narrative voice'. Further, there is a sense that everyday language works through metaphor, and an opportunity thus arises for an exploration of the nature of figurative colloquial language in diverse cultural contexts: poetry, as language working hard, can provide a springboard into various aspects of study. Sometimes the forms of the poems themselves derive from different cultural sources, and this, too, can be helpful. Anglo-Saxon *Kennings*, for example, work by shocking the reader into seeing something through its function, and then there are *Haiku*, tightly formed Japanese poems suggestive of a flash of insight.

I have been freely using the term 'intercultural' in the hope that implicit meaning may accrue, and the semantic field consequently broaden – that is, after all, the way that language generally works, especially, perhaps, in the educational context. But it is vital also that the nature of the inter-cultural project is brought into sharp focus. There is a danger that, otherwise, it may simply mean all things to all people, underlying any inter-personal encounter – which in a way of course it does – but thus losing any particular insight into educational practice. Any classroom inevitably comprises many and varied cultures, teachers and learners each being multi-faceted in this respect, and operates also within a whole series of broad and narrower cultural contexts, from the international to the specifically local. Essentially, the intercultural perspective is founded on a recognition of, wholehearted engagement with and, ultimately, a celebration of this state of affairs, while acknowledging the inevitable inherent tensions and their often problematic resolution. The school classroom, with its possible tradi-tional implications of a homogenous, teacher-centred monoculture, may perhaps be better construed as a workshop, embodying differentiation in inclusive practice – to use two terms very much in pedagogical vogue. Interestingly, such developments within the Literacy Strategy as Group- and Guided-Reading, and the general move towards ICT in its broadest sense as explored by McGuinn in Chapter 5, could be seen as part of this prac-tice, in that they imply a large measure of pupil-based independent learning on the basis of trust. Sometimes, the intercultural initiative demands a new way of looking even at imposed pedagogy, seeking opportunities for posi-tive, radical change where, on first sight, a threat may be more obvious. The way is, perhaps, open for imaginative initiatives centred on teaching and learning, such as those fostered by the Society for the Advancement of Philosophical Enquiry and Reflection in Education (SAPERE), who have as their guiding principle a quotation from a ten-year-old girl, Ellie: 'Philosophy relaxes me. If I'm worried, how can I learn anything? Because the class will respect my opinion, I can be myself and even change my mind without being laughed at.' Even a cursory glance at the work of SAPERE (www.sapere.net) will demonstrate the appropriateness of their projects to the intercultural vision – not least, in the present context, in the number and range of specifically English-focused ideas.

Not that there is any lack of possible threats to open teaching and learning also, some of which we have already glanced at. But the threats to an intercultural education really make its development all the more urgent. Clearly, and in my view rightly, there has been and is now a great deal of emphasis on the culture of schooling. In part at least, however, this has derived from managerial theories geared to making economic organisations work efficiently – hardly an aim likely to endear itself to Romantically inclined English teachers. New head teachers of schools deemed to be in the doldrums, for example, are expected efficiently and positively to 'turn round' the culture of their schools, on an industrial model. Although there are, frequently, highly desirable elements in this outlook – nobody, after all, could achieve much within a culture of failure, whatever that is – we have, at the same time, to be guarded about precisely what sorts of culture are intended here. If there is, in effect, a narrowing of identity, then this would be the very opposite of the intercultural project. Jones, in his aptly titled paper 'Culture Reinvented as Management' (2003) has helpfully outlined three features of what he calls 'the new culture of schooling' (2003: 148), locating these firmly in theories of new managerialism. Baldly, these are: first, an unquestioning attitude towards officially inspired or approved educational processes; second, a profound lack of interest or involvement in other people's experiences or cultures; and, finally, an avoidance or dismissal of extrinsic social or cultural factors and conditions in favour of emphasis on internal school policies geared towards effectively meeting targets. Evidently, there is little here to welcome in a radical intercultural context. Jones concludes that:

> Under the impact of the national curriculum/testing, the decline of teacher autonomy, and the attenuation of links between aspects of the work of the school and the activity of social and cultural movements, cultural connectedness is no longer important to the practice of English teaching. What has replaced them is . . . a curriculum based on the idea of 'entitlement' and 'access'. In current educational discourse, these terms carry a positive inflection. But it is worth considering also their quieter, and lethal, side. The terms signify the extinction of earlier, cultural-relativist models of teaching and learning; they register the predominance in the curriculum of a single type of authorised know-ledge. The role of the school is to ensure that students can successfully access this authorised form. . . . Since curriculum experiment and 'dialogue' around the validity of different forms of knowledge are less available options, teachers' work is channelled along other routes.
>
> (2003: 149)

Clearly, this analysis presents a picture antithetical to the intercultural perspective recommended here, and there does, indeed, seem to be some validity in the perception. However, it is our professional experience which strongly suggests that in countless English classrooms – and in schools generally – a rather different approach is taken: one far more in tune with an intercultural venture, at once subversive and dedicated to effective teaching. Assuredly, what is urgently needed, though, is a struggle (of which this book may be part) for the appropriate theoretical framework to allow this venture to flourish and develop.

We are back to the issue of particularity, in effect: as Eagleton maintains (2000: 78): 'For socialist thought, universality is inherent in the local, not an alternative to it' – and for 'socialist' we may read 'intercultural.' Eagleton, in his illuminating study of the nature of culture, goes on to quote Mulhern (2000: 80) emphasising that communities are 'not *places* but *practices* of collective identification whose variable order largely defines the culture of any actual social formation'. For English teaching, however, both *place* (in the expanded sense described in Chapter 2) and *practice* are hugely significant, and lie at the heart of the intercultural outlook. The two are neatly merged in an official Council of Europe statement on global education and democracy in schools – the sense of universality inherent in the local is clear here:

> Democracy is best learned in a democratic setting where participation is encouraged, where views can be expressed openly and discussed, where there is freedom of expression for pupils and teachers, and where there is fairness and justice. An appropriate climate is, therefore, an essential complement to effective learning about human rights.
>
> (Council of Europe 1996: 15)

Such proclamations, of course, are easily made – but, in practice, the implications are profound. Issues of citizenship, critical literacy and the intercultural perspective, it seems to me, are all crucial here. It also seems to me that, in my experience, of all places in schools it is the English classroom that has the clearest potential to realise such an education. Peim amplifies this point (2003: 31–32):

> English teaching both represents and enacts ideas about culture and language. . . . English occupies a special place . . . in relation to both culture and language. . . . [It] retains a central role in the curriculum and is at the core of issues around culture and values,

concluding that 'language and culture are continuous', as indeed they are, and demonstrably so.

It may be possible, gradually but more clearly, to see what this sort of continuity may mean in practice – and the act of seeing is, here, a potentially visionary act, in the sense that seeing a way forward and an ultimate goal enables the practitioner to walk purposefully, making a real difference to the immediate cultural context. This may be idealistic, in one sense, but it is not unrealistically so: the vision is embedded in everyday pedagogical practice. As the Italian anarchist Errico Malatesta (1982) maintained, in a different but certainly not totally irrelevant context, 'the subject is not whether we accomplish anarchism today, tomorrow, or within ten centuries, but that we walk towards anarchism today, tomorrow, and always'. The alternative is an abstract, ultimately vacuous idealism, the danger of which, in educational terms, has long been pointed out by radical commentators: Chanan and Gilchrist, for example (1974: 123–124), see that, all too often:

> Our values are permeated by an abstract idea of change or progress, instead of a progressively refined image of the condition we want to progress to. In the deification of the idea of progress man [*sic*] is distracted from his capacity for fulfilment in this world just as much as he was in the middle ages by the idea of the hereafter. It deflects him ... from the relatively short-term motivations which are the real springs of *chosen* social change.

This is an essentially intercultural perspective, and yet, as the very term 'intercultural' implies, the global dimension is equally significant. At a time when global cultural clashes are constantly threatening human peaceful co-existence – perhaps it was ever thus – it is all the more incumbent upon teachers – especially native language teachers, paradoxically – to develop an intercultural pedagogy. In the aftermath of the war against Iraq of 2003, Said has offered a powerful analysis of the international situation as it affects education – and, hopefully, as education of the right sort may affect it. Said draws a distinction between two opposing views of what learning about other cultures, at all levels from the particulars of the classroom outwards, may look like, asserting that

> there is a difference between knowledge of other peoples and other times that is the result of understanding, compassion, careful study and analysis for their own sakes, and on the other hand knowledge that is part of an overall campaign of self-affirmation.
>
> (Said 2003: 4)

Understandably, intercultural perspectives have, hitherto, focused largely on foreign language and culture teaching, resulting in the curious term 'intercultural competence', but the fundamental principles – even, or perhaps especially, in their developmental stage – strike me as especially apt for native language teaching. Fundamental to the entire project is the notion of Critical Pedagogy (CP), as outlined by intercultural theorists and practitioners such as Apple, Byram, Freire, Giroux, McLaren and Guilherme. For Guilherme (2002: 17), Critical Pedagogy

> supplies us with some pedagogical perspectives and processes, ... namely reflection, dissent, difference, dialogue, empowerment, action

and hope . . . . [It] is a pedagogy that includes teaching understood as part of the teaching/learning process viewed as the dialectical and dialogical reproduction and production of knowledge.

The radical, subversive relevance to the English classroom should begin to be clear, in that it combines what Giroux has called (1997: xii) the 'language of critique' with the 'language of possibility'. It is precisely this combination that is so important: either one without the other would be severely deficient – wholly negative, or purely idealistic. The intercultural teacher's role is to balance these elements, managing the necessary dialectical tension between them. Seeing the word and the world (Freire's telling fusion) as new, open to critical insight *and* a sense of wonder, to critical distance *and* informed engagement, is absolutely fundamental here, and is at the heart of what this book is recommending. The implication is that knowledge and understanding are there to be unlearned and relearned as well as learned. This does not refer simply to curricular knowledge, but to the very stuff of the relationship between those engaged in teaching and learning. As so often, there is a kernel of good teaching common sense in this: all teachers must surely acknowledge, explicitly or otherwise, that the success of their particular classroom depends on its culture – specifically the tension between modes of social behaviour accrued through experience and brought to the classroom, and those negotiated, formed and learned as a direct result of being there. Somehow or other, good teaching manages this tension, in both enabling and directing senses of good management, with varying degrees of theoretical self-consciousness.

This is where the subversive dimension comes in, as the kind of educational experience implied here is manifestly about power – about who has it, and what is done with it to whom – whether in macrocosmic or microcosmic context. Whereas for traditional schooling notions of power are rarely brought to the fore, and any inadvertent teaching about or through power structures does nothing to question their nature, except perhaps in very generalised terms, for the intercultural teacher the nature of these structures is central, manifest – and necessarily subversive. The form of the subversion may be in the culture of the classroom itself, manifesting itself in the open, debated acknowledgement of inter-subjectivities and social relations, as well as in the content of the curriculum, as exemplified in study of such texts as *Hamlet* and *Subterranean Homesick Blues* outlined in Chapter 1. Intercultural teaching and learning is effectively a form of Critical Pedagogy. As Guilherme elaborates:

Critical Pedagogy (CP) . . . intervenes with ways of knowing and ways of living thus being a cultural enterprise as well as an educational one. CP deals with the relationship between the self, the others and the world and by leading the pupils to critically examine these relationships it makes them believe that they can make a difference and, in so doing, the pedagogical and the cultural become political too.

(2002: 21)

The link between critical thought and interculturism is a strong one – indeed, the two are ultimately interdependent, as Said (2003: 6) makes clear:

> Critical thought does not submit to commands to join in the ranks marching against one or another approved enemy. Rather than the manufactured clash of civilisations, we need to concentrate on the slow working together of cultures that overlap, borrow from each other, and live together.

Said's resolution of this need is through a form of humanism which 'is centred upon the agency of human individuality and subjective intuition, rather than on received ideas and authority'. And the subject English, whether textually oriented or otherwise, seems peculiarly suited to aiming at fulfilment of this need.

The role of the teacher – specifically the English teacher – is, as I have argued throughout, absolutely central to this project. But, by the same token, the intercultural teacher, as does any effective artist, knows when to step back, when to give space. Official pronouncements on the nature of teaching, including the Teacher Training Agency Standards for initial teacher training and subsequent professional development, tend to give the impression of the teacher as a stable, dominant, sovereign and controlling fixed entity – or at least that is what teachers are supposed to aspire to. In reality, the situation is rather different, as MacIntyre wryly puts it: 'among the central moral fictions of our age we have to place the peculiarly managerial fiction embodied in the claim to possess systematic effectiveness in controlling certain aspects of social reality' (1985: 74).

Intercultural teaching – Critical Pedagogy – acknowledges and embraces this difference, as it does all difference. This is its intercultural core: a recognition and celebration of negotiated, complex relationships of teaching and learning. To return to the metaphor of place, recurrent in this argument, Gregoriou (2001: 135) notes that

> a philosophical investigation of place from a pedagogical perspective asks how we *make place* for others: how we receive what is abstract and unintelligible, how we expand the borders of our localities and soften the ligaments of our ethnic, historical and cultural identities so that we can envelope new discursive idioms and narratives in the genealogies of our cultures.

Especially noteworthy here is the emphasis placed on pluralities – of identity, of culture, of others – suggestive of a definitively intercultural classroom. The particular flavour of the subject English, I suggest, derives partly from the same sources, especially the cultural, and partly from the proposed envelopment of specifically discursive idioms and narratives – the very stuff of an imaginatively conceived English curriculum.

Perhaps we are beginning, with these kinds of perception, to form a tentative answer to the challenge of how to see literacy in ways which are both realistic for the classroom, and profoundly radical – the challenge as provocatively put by commentators like Hoyles a generation ago:

> Most of the time we don't question the purpose of literacy. In school its function so often seems simply one of social control. If it is to be liberating, the problem is how to *change* the context. . . . The problem is how to revolutionise the *total* context.
>
> (Hoyles 1977: 30)

In order to offer some sort of working resolution of this question, there needs to be genuine pedagogical reflection, and this, again, is part of the intercultural world-view – in the sense that Dewey first suggested as the basis of his theory of democratic education:

> reflective thinking, in distinction from other operations to which we apply the name of thought, involves (1) a state of doubt, hesitation, perplexity, mental difficulty, in which thinking originates, and (2) an act of searching, hunting, inquiring, to find material that will resolve the doubt, settle and dispose of the perplexity.
>
> (1933: 12)

Again, the similarity to Romantic thought is striking and, again, such a perception seems particularly relevant to the teaching of English, frequently alone among the core curricular subjects in its emphasis on the processes of perception in learning as opposed to the acquisition of a vast body of information in the guise of 'knowledge'.

As Medway (2002: 6) elaborates:

> The needed epistemology of English . . . must go on to specify that English doesn't teach about the world in the way that Biology does. Rather than accounts that aspire to be objective in the sense that they record what is potentially available to any investigator, English typically deals with phenomenological knowledge; knowledge of the world *as it enters experience*. This is Bruner's point about the 'subjectivisation' that is characteristic of literary texts, novels and films.

Dewey himself emphasised the dynamic triangular nature of learning in the sense outlined here, involving knowledge-as-perception, experience, and reflective thinking. Guilherme elucidates (2002: 28):

> Dewey saw the relationship between theory and practice as a web that is continuously made and remade. Furthermore, he saw the connection between experience and learning as part of a wider democratic project that linked education and society. . . . This triangular mode of learning would provide young individuals with the attitudes and skills necessary for the reinforcement of a democratic way of life and would also empower them to take advantage of all the possibilities they have access to while living in a democratic society.

Subsequent radicalisation and extension of Dewey's arguments, to encompass political and social as well as pedagogical dimensions of struggle, by Williams, Freire and Eagleton among many others, have further strengthened their validity in the intercultural context. The fusion of inter-cultural and pedagogical insights is, indeed, striking: issues of culture and issues of the classroom tend to model, complement and create friction between each other. In the following perceptive quotation from Williams, for example, the word 'teaching' could quite easily – and tellingly – be substituted for 'culture', and the reciprocity serves to illuminate both:

> We have to plan what can be planned, according to our common deci-sion. But the emphasis of the idea of culture is right when it reminds us that a culture, essentially, is unplannable. We have to ensure the means of life, and the means of community. But what will then, by these means, be lived, we cannot know or say. The idea of culture rests on a metaphor: the tending of natural growth. And indeed it is on growth, as metaphor and as fact, that the ultimate emphasis must be placed.
>
> (in Eagleton 2000: 119–120)

It is precisely this sort of formulation which provides a key to unlocking the nature of the culture of the classroom.

From this kind of perspective, the urgent need to keep re-invigorating language is hardly a luxury. It is, rather, at the very core of our project as English teachers. As George Orwell realised and illustrated so frighteningly in *Nineteen Eighty-Four*, control over language means power. The 'Ingsoc' tyranny portrayed in the novel developed 'Newspeak' – a term that, inter-estingly, has entered popular consciousness – precisely so that 'a heretical thought – that is, a thought diverging from the principles of Ingsoc – should be literally unthinkable, at least so far as thought is dependent on words'

(Orwell 1949: 312). For many, inside and outside our classrooms, this is no merely academic matter, as Kureishi observes:

> It is always illuminating to think of those groups and individuals who are denied the privilege of speaking and of being listened to, whether they be immigrants, asylum seekers, women, the mad, children, the elderly, or workers in the third world. It is where the words end, or can't go, that abuse takes place, whether it's racial harassment, bullying, neglect, or sexual violence.
>
> (2003: 4)

One of the objects portrayed from a Martian viewpoint in the previously cited poem *A Martian Sends a Postcard Home* is, clearly, a car. The sense of child-like wonder at the endless picture-show seen from inside the car is vividly evoked. Seen from another point of view, however, there is rather less to celebrate in the car and all the commercial and industrial baggage that comes with it: in a sense this is the distinction between the vantage points of innocence and of experience. Interestingly, Heathcote Williams in his poem *Autogeddon* uses the same 'Martian' conceit as does Raine, but with a quite different outcome: highly political and intensely critical of the domination of the car in our society. It is a long, often quite complex poem, but even in the brief excerpt below both the similarity and contrast to *A Martian* . . . are abundantly plain. A version of the work was made for the BBC TV programme *Forty Minutes*, presented by the actor Jeremy Irons and using a wide range of audio and visual footage to amplify the poem's message – and very powerfully too.

. . . Were an Alien Visitor
To hover a few hundred yards above the planet
It could be forgiven for thinking
That cars were the dominant life-form,
And that human beings were a kind of ambulatory fuel cell,
Injected when the car wished to move off
And ejected when they were spent . . .

. . . Listen, on a good day,
Three cars are manufactured for every child born,
One per second world-wide,
And we need every kid you can manufacture
To fill em . . .

. . . The healing landscape,
In which the human spirit could re-tune itself,

Had been violated by a million million cars
Since the century began.

Cars' nitrogen-oxide waste,
Acting deceptively as air-borne fertiliser,
Persuaded trees it was still the growing season . . .

. . . Their lungs the oxygenating leaves withered;
pine needles grew grey, metallic tips
And dropped to the ground . . .
In Switzerland the forests were so flimsy
Avalanches tore through them as though they were straw.

As the planet was slowly shaved of cleansing tree-cover,
Air, the Visitor observed,
could come in as short-winded supply
As the breath of a sedentary driver.

In Rome, the traffic police went on strike,
Claiming they were unable to breathe.
In Japan, department stores were selling oxygen,
Dispensing it in purpose-built bars . . .

Children wheeled past exhaust pipes at chest level
Become catalytic converters . . .
. . . As cars reconditioned the air,
Usurping the elements,
Threatening to become the weather . . .
The earth's self-regulator
Had pulled the plug
And allowed the thin coat of protection
That had given humanity its life
To open up.

More than seventeen million people have been killed on the roads since
the motor car first appeared. An incalculable number have been seriously
hurt. In the future, half the world is likely to be run over in a terminal
squabble for oil. For today we are possessed by a mindless monster
which threatens the planet itself.

From *Autogeddon*, Heathcote Williams

Again, I have used this poem with remarkable success in the classroom, either independently or as complementary to (and contrasting with) *A Martian* . . . . The *Forty Minutes* presentation is essentially an intertextual, multi-media, highly persuasive version of the poem, incorporating extracts from TV car ads, archive film footage, music, snatches of soap-type dialogue among many other elements. As such, it may be used as an appropriate model for students' own experiments with media-based persuasive texts, cutting across genres in a vividly exciting way and giving the notion of performance poetry an inventive breadth. Because of this potential, teaching the poem may be said to blend a 'language of critique' with a 'language of possibility', to use Freire's and Giroux's intercultural terms. Guilherme elaborates further on this potentially telling combination:

> A language of critique entails a critical understanding of society as it is, with different layers of meaning and with several forces in interaction. . . . It involves a deconstructive view of reality and a challenge to fixed interpretive frames. . . . A language of possibility results . . . from the urge to explore new alternatives, to envision a revitalisation of democratic ideals and to engage in social change. . . . The combination of a language of critique with a language of possibility turns education into a form of cultural politics.
>
> (2002: 34)

This sort of valuable, value-laden and challenging insight may be given particularly sharp focus in the English classroom through the creative use of texts such as *Autogeddon*, which, in a sense, models through its intertextuality and critical questioning the very qualities recommended as characteristic of the intercultural classroom.

I should like to round off this chapter by looking at one more Blake text: the *Song of Experience* (no text could be more centred on the meanings of Blakean experience) simply entitled *London*. As it is so richly fertile, yet concise, it is worth quoting here in full (see facing page).

A great deal could be – and has been – written about this poem, from all sorts of angles. My purpose here, however, is to explore it as richly emblematic of the Romantic intercultural project for education. The first point to make is that, like many suggestive texts, it is both worth teaching and simultaneously worth learning from in the context of pedagogy: the poet/narrator may be likened to the teacher, in effect, and in this sense the poem models positive reciprocity. Particularly striking in this respect is the dynamic combination of critical detachment from the observed situation, and passionate involvement in it – the detachment making possible a startling clarity of vision, balanced by the powerfully felt motivation to do something about it. It is precisely this combination that has been recommended throughout this book; the two qualities are complementary in an

I wander through each chartered street
Near where the chartered Thames does flow
And mark in every face I meet
Marks of weakness, marks of woe.

In every cry of every man
In every infant's cry of fear
In every voice, in every ban
The mind-forged manacles I hear.

How the chimney-sweeper's cry
Every blackening church appals
And the hapless soldier's sigh
Runs in blood down palace walls.

But most through midnight streets I hear
How the youthful harlot's curse
Blasts the new-born infant's tear
And blights with plagues the marriage hearse.

intercultural context, and neither would be sufficient by itself. Although part of the same oppressive world he depicts in the poem, Blake, by virtue of his poetic insight, is able to penetrate it critically; by doing this he implies a way forward.

There are various further relevant dimensions arising from *London*. I am struck by the fusion of senses, especially sight and hearing, and the way Blake plays so skilfully on the intense relationship between the particular – the three increasingly hapless figures of the chimney-sweeper, the soldier and the young prostitute – and the universal qualities their oppression denotes. Microcosmic and macrocosmic realities are evocatively fused here, in the same way that the classroom both reflects wider realities and forms its own particular version. The language of the poem may be seen as an exercise in critical literacy: I can think of no better way of linking word, sentence and text level studies than through the exploration of *London*. The contexts of the poem, ranging from its place as a song of experience in the wider collection of the *Songs of Innocence and of Experience* to its social, political and psychological interpretative possibilities, offer great scope for further meaningful analysis. It is, in essence, a radical study of urban alienation – spiritual, sexual, social and political – given startling immediacy through Blake's compressed poetic visionary imagination. The English classroom, although thankfully unlikely to contain quite such glaring instances of oppression, may well be helpfully seen 'through' (Blake's formulation) the same eyes.

But, most of all, I am interested in the 'mind-forged manacles' Blake hears in all the sounds of London. Manacles they are, to all intents and purposes, but in seeing their 'mind-forged' nature the poet suggests the subtle connection between social reality and consciousness, objectivity and subjectivity, cause and effect. In effect, this is a vivid evocation of what Habermas called the 'intersubjectively recognised subject', transcending the false, and unhelpful, dichotomy between 'outer' and 'inner' worlds and words. Kureishi elucidates further on the linguistic essence of the 'mind-forged manacles', describing

> the person who doesn't want to hear their own words. This is the person who owns them, who has made them inside his own body, but who both does, and does not, have access to them, who is prisoner, prison and the law. Real dictators in the world are a picture, too, of dictators within individuals, of certain kinds of minds.
>
> (2003: 5)

The teaching of English should have as its central aim the liberation of this manacled world, and the starting point may well be the minute particulars of the classroom – including the manacles, mind-forged or otherwise – to be found there.

Notes

3 Romantic words and worlds

1 The quotations from David Holbrook cited in this chapter are taken from the Seminar Papers of the Dartmouth Conference.

2 As early as 1886, the Cross Commission lent official support to Froebel's belief that pupil motivation and an element of play should be regarded as important elements in the teaching of writing in schools.

3 These four pre-1914 texts appeared on the Key Stage 3 English SAT papers for 2003. The three plays were set for the Shakespeare Paper. *Treasure Island* featured on the Reading Paper.

4 The non-fictional text types described in the National Literacy Strategy are: information, recount, explanation, instruction, persuasion and discursive writing.

4 The challenge of 'instrumental rationality'

1 Chris Smith was, at the time, Secretary of State for Culture, Media and Sport.

2 Key Stage 3 SATs are compulsory for state school pupils working above National Curriculum Level 3.

3 Figures taken from *The Independent*, 10 September 2003.

4 Kress was writing here before the National Literacy Strategy – with its emphasis upon alternatives to the 'poetic' and 'literary' genres – was introduced into the school curriculum.

5 The passage is reproduced here as it was originally spelt and punctuated.

6 See the reference to Geoffrey Hill's poem *September Song* in the previous chapter.

7 Directed by James Britton, the Schools Council's Writing Across the Curriculum Project of the 1970s classified writing into three types: 'poetic' (relating to the language of the arts and literature); 'transactional' (relating to factual statements); and 'expressive' (relating to personal and 'creative' writing).

8 *Elegy 2: To his Mistress Going to Bed.*

9 The quotation is taken from Keats' *Ode to a Nightingale.*

10 Ariel had been imprisoned in a tree by the witch Sycorax and subsequently released by Prospero when he arrived on the island. Prospero uses the threat of re-imprisonment to ensure Ariel's obedience.

5   'Taking the mind to other things'

1   The words 'and Communication' (ICT) had not been added to the title at the time when Sally Tweddle was writing.
2   Blacker and McKie's thought-provoking essay, *Information and Communication Technology*, provided the starting-point for many of the ideas explored in this chapter.
3   Quotations from the boys' emails are reproduced as spelt and punctuated.
4   Like many English teachers, I am indebted to the practical work undertaken by Trevor Millum and Chris Warren in this area.

Bibliography

Abbs, P. (1976) *Root and Blossom: Essays on the Philosophy, Practice and Politics of English Teaching*, London: Heinemann

Abbs, P. (1982) *English within the Arts: A Radical Alternative for English and the Arts in the Curriculum*, London: Hodder and Stoughton

Alred, G., Byram, M. and Fleming, M. (eds) (2003) *Intercultural Experience and Education*, Clevedon: Multilingual Matters

Andrews, R. (1997) 'Editorial: Electronic English', *English in Education*, 31 (2): 1–3

Andrews, R. (2001) *Teaching and Learning English: A Guide to Recent Research and its Applications*, London: Continuum

Ash, R. (2000) *The Top 10 of Everything: 2001*, London: Dorling Kindersley

Astley, N. (2002) 'Introduction', in N. Astley (ed.) *Stating Alive: Real Poems for Unreal Times*, Tarset: Bloodaxe Books

Auden, W. H. (1963) *The Dyer's Hand and Other Essays*, London: Faber and Faber

Babbage, J. and McGuinn, N. (2000) *Using Email to Assist Reading*, London: TTA Publications

Bain, R. (1991) *Reflections: Talking about Language*, London: Hodder and Stoughton

Bartlett, S., Burton, D. and Peim, N. (2001) *Introduction to Educational Studies*, London: Paul Chapman Publishing

Baumann, A. S., Bloomfield, A. and Roughton, L. (1997) *Becoming a Secondary School Teacher*, London: Hodder and Stoughton

Blacker, D. and McKie, J. (2003) 'Information and Communication Technology', in N. Blake, P. Smeyers, R. Smith and P. Standish (eds) *The Blackwell Guide to the Philosophy of Education*, Oxford: Blackwell Publishing

Blake, W. (ed. Stevens 1995) *Selected Works*, Cambridge: Cambridge University Press

Blishen, E. (1978) *Sorry, Dad: An Autobiography*, London: Hamish Hamilton

Boal, A. (1992) *Games for Actors and Non-Actors*, London and New York: Routledge

Boden, M. (2001) 'Creativity and Knowledge', in A. Craft, B. Jeffrey and M. Leibling (eds) *Creativity in Education*, London: Continuum

Boltor, J. D. (1991) *Writing Space: The Computer, Hypertext, and the History of Writing*, Hillsdale, NJ: Erlbaum

Bourdieu, P. (1991) *Language and Symbolic Power*, Cambridge: Polity Press

Bourne, G. ([1923] 1963) *The Wheelwright's Shop*, Cambridge: Cambridge University Press

Bowers, C. A. (1982) 'The Reproduction of Technological Consciousness: Locating the Ideological Foundations of a Radical Pedagogy', *Teacher College Record*, 83 (4): 529–557

Bowker, J. (ed.) (1991) *Secondary Media Education: A Curriculum Statement*, London: British Film Institute

Bowles, S. and Gintis, H. (1976) *Schooling in Capitalist America: Educational Reform and the Contradictions of Economic Life*, London: Routledge and Kegan Paul

Brindley, S. (ed.) (1994) *Teaching English*, London: Routledge

Britton, J. (1972) *Language and Learning*, Harmondsworth: Pelican Books

Brooker, P. (1994) 'Key words in Brecht's theory and practice of theatre', in P. Thomson and G. Sacks (eds) *The Cambridge Companion to Brecht*, Cambridge: Cambridge University Press

Brown, S. and McIntyre, D. (1993) *Making Sense of Teaching*, Buckingham: Open University Press

Bruner, J. (1971) 'The Perfectibility of Intellect', in A. Gil (ed.) *The Relevance of Education*, New York: W. W. Norton and Company

Bruner, J. S., Jolly, A. and Sylva, K. (1976) (eds) *Play: Its Role in Development and Evolution*, Harmondsworth: Penguin

Burgess, T., Fox, C. and Goody, J. (2002) *'When the Hurly Burly's Done': What's Worth Fighting for in English Education*, Sheffield: NATE

Callaghan, J. (1976) 'Towards a National Debate: Text of the Prime Minister's Ruskin Speech' *Education*, 22 October, pp. 332–333

Carlyle, T. ([1843] 1915) *Past and Present*, Boston: Richard D. Altick

Carr, D. (2003) *Making Sense of Education*, London: Routledge Falmer

Carter, R. (1995) *Keywords in Language and Literacy*, London and New York: Routledge

Chambers, A. (1985) *Tell Me: Children, Reading and Talk*, Stroud: Thimble Press

Chanan, G. and Gilchrist, L. (1974) *What School is For*, London: Methuen

Cliff-Hodges, G., Drummond, M. J. and Styles, M. (eds) (2000) *Tales, Tellers and Texts*, London: Cassell

Cohen, J. (ed.) (1999) *Educating Hearts and Minds*, New York: Teachers College Press

Cook, C. (1917) *The Play Way*, London: Heinemann

Council of Europe (1996) *Modern Languages: Learning, Teaching, Assessment. A Common European Framework of Reference*, Strasbourg: Council of Europe

Cox, B. (1991) *Cox on Cox: An English Curriculum for the 1990s*, London: Hodder and Stoughton

Craft, A., Jeffrey, B. and Leibling, M. (eds) (2001) *Creativity in Education*, London: Continuum

Creber, J. W. Patrick (1972) *Lost for Words: Language and Educational Failure*, Harmondsworth: Penguin

Csikszentmihalyi, M. (1990) *Flow*, London: HarperCollins

D'Arcy, P. (2000) *Two Contrasting Paradigms for the Teaching and Assessment of Writing*, Sheffield: NATE

Davies, I., Gregory, I. and McGuinn, N. (2002) *Key Debates in Education*, London: Continuum

Davison, J. and Moss, J. (eds) (2000) *Issues in English Teaching*, London: Routledge

Day, A. (1996) *Romanticism: The New Critical Idiom*, London: Routledge

Dean, G. (2000) *Teaching Reading in Secondary Schools*, London: David Fulton

de Bono, E. (1996) *Textbook of Wisdom*, London: Penguin

Dentith, S. (1995) *Bakhtinian Thought: An Introductory Reader*, London: Routledge

DES (1975) *A Language for Life*, London: HMSO

DES (1989) *English for Ages 5–16* (Cox Report), London: HMSO

DES/WO (1993) *English for Ages 5 to 16*, London: HMSO

Dewey, J. ([1925] 1981) 'Experience and Nature', in J. A. Boydston (ed.) *John Dewey: The Later Works*, vol. 1, Carbondale: Southern Illinois University Press

Dewey, J. (1933) *How to Think*, Boston: D. C. Heath

DfEE (1998) *The National Literacy Strategy: Framework for Teaching*, Sudbury: DfEE Publications

DfEE (1999) *A Fresh Start: Improving Literacy and Numeracy*, Sudbury: DfEE Publications

DfEE/QCA (1999) *English: The National Curriculum for English*, London: DfEE and QCA Publications

DfEE (2000) *Research Topic Paper 1: Race Research for the Future: Ethnicity in Education, Training and the Labour Market*, Nottingham: DfEE Publications

DfEE (2001) *Key Stage 3 National Strategy: Framework for Teaching English Years 7, 8 and 9*, London: HMSO

Dickinson, P. (1992) *A Bone from a Dry Sea*, London: Corgi Freeway

Dixon, J. (1967) *Growth Through English*, Oxford: Oxford University Press

Dylan, B. (1987) *Lyrics 1962–1985*, London: Jonathan Cape

Dymoke, S. (2003) *Drafting and Assessing Poetry*, London: Paul Chapman

Eagleton, T. (2000) *The Idea of Culture*, Oxford: Blackwell

Ellis, V. (2002) 'Introduction' to Pullman, P. *Perverse, All Monstrous, All Prodigious Things*, Sheffield: NATE

Ellul, J. (1964) *The Technological Society*, (trans. J Wilkinson) New York: Vintage Books

Feenberg, A. (1991) *A Critical Theory of Technology*, New York: Oxford University Press

Fischer, E. (ed.) (1973) *Marx in His Own Words*, Harmondsworth: Penguin

Fleming, M. and Stevens, D. (1998) *English Teaching in the Secondary School*, London: David Fulton

Fowles, J. (1981) *The Aristos* (rev. edn), Reading: Triad

Freire, P. (1970; this edn 1996) *Pedagogy of the Oppressed*, London: Penguin

Freire, P. (1990) *Pedagogy of the Oppressed*, New York: Continuum

Freire, P. and Macedo, D. (1987) *Literacy: Reading the Word and the World*, South Hadley, MA: Bergin and Garvey Publishers

Friel, B. (1981) *Translations*, London: Faber and Faber

Gale, T. and Densmore, K. (2000) *Just Schooling: Explorations in the Cultural Politics of Teaching*, Buckingham: Open University Press

Gardner, H. (1993) *Frames of Mind: The Theory of Multiple Intelligences*, New York: Basic Books

Gibson, R. (1984) *Structuralism and Education*, London: Hodder and Stoughton

Giroux, H. (1997) *Pedagogy and the Politics of Hope: Theory, Culture and Schooling*, Boulder, CO: Westview Press

Goodwyn, A. (1992) 'English Teachers and the Cox Models', *English in Education*, 28 (3): 4–10

Goodwyn, A. (ed.) (1998) *Literary and Media Texts in Secondary English: New Approaches*, London: Cassell

Goodwyn, A. (ed.) (2000) *English in the Digital Age: Information and Communications Technology and the Teaching of English*, London and New York: Cassell

Goodwyn, A. (ed.) (2002) *Improving Literacy at KS2 and KS3*, London: Paul Chapman

Goodwyn, A., Adams, A. and Clarke, S. (1997) 'The Great God of the Future: Views of Current and Future English Teachers on the Place of IT in English', *English in Education*, 31 (2): 54–62

Green, B. (ed.) (1993) *The Insistence of the Letter: Literacy Studies and Curriculum Theorising*, London: Falmer

Gregoriou, Z. (2001) 'Does Speaking of Others Involve Receiving the Other?', in G. Biesta and Egea-Kuehne (eds) *Derrida and Education*, London: Routledge

Guilherme, M. (2002) *Critical Citizens for an Intercultural World*, Clevedon: Multilingual Matters

Habermas, J. (1970) *Towards a Rational Society*, Boston: Beacon Press

Hardman, F. (2001) 'What Do We Mean by Secondary English Teaching?', in J. Williamson, M. Fleming, F. Hardman and D. Stevens, *Meeting the Standards in Secondary English: A Guide to the ITT NC*, London and New York: Routledge/Falmer

Hardman, F. and Williamson, J. (1993) 'Student Teachers and Models of English', *Journal of Education for Teaching*, 19 (3): 279–292

Hargreaves, A. and Goodson, I. (1996) *Teachers' Professional Lives*, London: Falmer Press

Hargreaves, D. (1999) 'The Knowledge-creating School', *British Journal of Educational Studies*, 47 (2): 123

Harrison, B. (1983) *English Studies 11–18: An Arts-based Approach*, London: Hodder and Stoughton

Harrison, B. (1994) *The Literate Imagination: Renewing the Secondary English Curriculum*, London: David Fulton

Harrison, C. *et al.* (1998) 'Multimedia Portables for Teachers Pilot: Project Report' Coventry: British Educational Communications and Technology Agency

Harrison, M. and Stuart-Clark, C. (eds) (1989) *Peace and War: A Collection of Poems*, Oxford: Oxford University Press

Harrison, T. (1978) *From the School of Eloquence and Other Poems*, London: Rex Collings

Heaney, S. (1980) *Preoccupations: Selected Prose 1968–1978*, London: Faber and Faber

Hill, G. (1968) *King Log*, London: André Deutsch

Hillocks Jr., G. (1999) *Ways of Thinking, Ways of Teaching*, New York: Teachers College Press

Hirsch, E. D. (2001) 'Romancing the Child', *Education Next*, Spring 2001: 14–25

HMSO (1921) *The Teaching of English in England*, London: HMSO

Hoare, Q. (1977) 'Education: Programmes and People', in Hoyles, M (ed.) *The Politics of Literacy*, London: Writers and Readers Publishing Cooperative

Holbrook, D. (1968) 'Creativity in the English Programme', in G. Summerfield (ed.) *Creativity in English*, National Council of Teachers of English

Holt, J. (1972) *Freedom and Beyond*, Harmondsworth: Penguin

Horkheimer, M. and Adorno, T. (1991) *Dialectic of Enlightenment*, New York: Continuum

Hornbrook, D. (1989) *Education and Dramatic Art*, Oxford: Blackwell Education

Hoyles, M. (1977) *The Politics of Literacy*, London: Writers and Readers Publishing Cooperative

Jeffcoate, R, (1992) *Starting English Teaching*, London and New York: Routledge

Johnston, J. (1987) *Shadows on our Skin*, London: Heinemann

Jones, K. (2003) 'Culture Reinvented as Management', *Changing English*, 10 (2): 143–155

Keane, F. (1996) *Letter to Daniel*, London: Penguin (and as a BBC Radio Collection audiotape: BBC Worldwide 1997)

Kress, G. (1994) *Learning to Write*, London and New York: Routledge

Kress, G. (1995) *Writing the Future: English and the Making of a Culture of Innovation*, Sheffield: NATE

Kureishi, H. (2003) 'Loose Tongues and Liberty' in *The Guardian*, (07/06/03)

Lanham, R. (1993) *The Electronic Word: Democracy, Technology and the Arts*, Chicago and London: University of Chicago Press

Lanham, R. (1996) 'The Electronic Word: Multimedia, Rhetoric and English Teaching' *The English and Media Magazine*, 35: 40–43

Lankshear, C. (1993) 'Curriculum as Literacy: Reading and Writing in "New Times"', in B. Green (ed.) *The Insistence of the Letter: Literacy Studies and Curriculum Theorising*, London: Falmer Press

Lankshear, C. (ed.) (1997) *Changing Literacies*, Buckingham: Open University Press

Laurel, B. (1991) *Computers as Theatre*, Reading, MA: Addison-Wesley

Lawlor, S. (1988) *Correct Core: Simple Curricula for English, Maths and Science*, London: Centre for Policy Studies

Lawrence, D. H. ([1920] 1960) *Women in Love*, Harmondsworth: Penguin

Lawrence, D. (1996) *Enhancing Self-esteem in the Classroom*, London: Paul Chapman

Leach, J. (1997) 'English Teachers "On-line": Developing a New Community of Discourse', *English in Education*, 31 (2): 63–72

Leach, J. (2001) 'A Hundred Possibilities: Creativity, Community and ICT', in A. Craft, B. Jeffrey and M. Leibling (eds) *Creativity in Education*, London: Continuum

Leavis, F. R. (1943) 'Why Universities?', in F. R. Leavis, *Education and the University: A Sketch for an 'English School'*, London: Chatto and Windus

Leavis, F. R. and Thompson, D. (1933) *Culture and Environment*, London: Chatto and Windus

Lefebvre, H. (1968) *The Sociology of Marx*, London: Allen Lane

Lewis, M. and Wray, D. (eds) (2000) *Literacy in the Secondary School*, London: David Fulton

Lister, I. (1973) 'Education, Politics and a Vision of Man: A Conversation with Paulo Freire'. Draft text of an article for *The Times Higher Education Supplement*, available from the Department of Educational Studies, University of York

Lucas, B. (2001) 'Creative Teaching, Teaching Creativity and Creative Learning' in A. Craft, B. Jeffrey and M. Leibling (eds) *Creativity in Education*, London: Continuum

Macedo, D. (1994) 'Preface'. In P. L. McLaren and C. Lankshear (eds) (1994) *Politics of Liberation: Paths from Freire*, London and New York: Routledge

McCormick, K. (1994) *The Culture of Reading and the Teaching of English*, Manchester: Manchester University Press

McGowan, H. (2002) *Schooling*, London: Faber and Faber

McGuinn, N. (1994) '"Enabling" or "Restriction"? the Reception of the English Order', in M. Bottery, C. Brock and M. Richmond (eds) *Politics and the Curriculum*, BCIES: University of Hull

McGuinn, N. (2001) 'Finding a Voice Through Email', in W. Frindte, T. Köhler, P. Marquet and E. Nissen (eds) *Internet-based Teaching and Learning (IN-TELE) 99*, Frankfurt am Main: Peter Lang

McGuinn, N. (2002) 'How and Why do we Learn?', in I. Davies, I. Gregory and N. McGuinn *Key Debates in Education*, London and New York: Continuum

MacIntyre, A. (1985) *After Virtue: A Study in Moral Theory*, London: Duckworth

McLaren, P. L. and Lankshear, C. (eds) (1994) *Politics of Liberation: Paths from Freire*, London and New York: Routledge

Malatesta, E. (1930; this edn 1982) *Towards Anarchism*, Edmonton: Black Cat Press

Marsh, J. and Millard, E. (2000) *Literacy and Popular Culture: Using Children's Culture in the Classroom*, London: Paul Chapman

Marshall, B. (2000) 'A Rough Guide to English Teachers', *English in Education*, 34 (1): 24–41

Marshall, B. (2001) 'Creating Danger: The Place of the Arts in Education Policy', in A. Craft, B. Jeffrey and M. Leibling (eds) *Creativity in Education*, London: Continuum

Marshall, B., Turvey, A. and Brindley, S. (2001) 'English Teachers – Born or Made: A Longitudinal Study on the Socialisation of English Teachers', *Changing English*, 8 (2): 189–203

Maslow, A. H. (1954) *Motivation and Personality*, New York: Harper and Row

Masterman, L. (1985) *Teaching the Media*, London and New York: Routledge

Mathieson, M. (1975) *The Preachers of Culture: A Study of English and its Teachers*, London: George Allen and Unwin

Medway, P. (1989) 'Argument as Social Action', in R. Andrews (ed.) *Narrative and Argument*, Milton Keynes: Open University Press

Medway, P. (2002) 'Show Him the Documents: Teaching and Learning the English Method', *The English and Media Magazine*, issue 47

Megill, A. (1985) *Prophets of Extremity*, Berkeley: University of California Press

Moore, A. (2000) *Teaching and Learning: Pedagogy, Curriculum and Culture*, London: RoutledgeFalmer

Mortimore, P. (ed.) (1999) *Understanding Pedagogy and its Impact on Learning*, London: Paul Chapman

Myhill, D. (1999) 'Writing Matters: Linguistic Characteristics of Writing in GCSE English Examinations', *English in Education*, 33 (3): 70–81

National Advisory Committee on Creative and Cultural Education (NACCCE) (2001) *All Our Futures: Creativity, Culture and Education*, London: DfEE

National Writing Project (1990) *Perceptions of Writing*, Walton-on-Thames: Nelson

Nobel, A. (1996) *Educating Through Art: The Steiner School Approach*, Edinburgh: Floris Books

Orwell, G. (1949) *Nineteen Eighty-Four*, Harmondsworth: Penguin

Papert, S. (1980) *Mindstorms: Children, Computers and Powerful Ideas*, New York: Basic Books

Peach, L. and Burton, A. (1995) *English as a Creative Art: Literary Concepts Linked to Creative Writing*, London: David Fulton

Pearson, G. (1983) *Hooligan*, London: Macmillan

Peel, R., Patterson, A. and Gerlach, J. (2000) *Questions of English*, London: RoutledgeFalmer

Peim, N. (1993) *Critical Theory and the English Teacher: Transforming the Subject*, London: Routledge

Peim, N. (2003) *Changing English? Rethinking the Politics of English Teaching*, Sheffield: NATE

Pike, M. (2004) *Teaching Secondary English*, London: Paul Chapman

Qualifications and Curriculum Authority (2003) *Sample English Test Shakespeare Paper: Macbeth*, London: Qualifications and Curriculum Authority

Read, H. (1958) *Education Through Art*, London: Faber and Faber

Richards, I. A. ([1924] 1935) *Principles of Literary Criticism*, London: Kegan Paul, Trench, Truber

Richards, I. A. (1929) *Practical Criticism*, London: Routledge and Kegan Paul

Rosen, H. (1992) 'The Politics of Writing', in K. Kimberley, M. Meek and J. Miller (eds) *New Readings: Contributions to an Understanding of Literacy*, London: A & C Black.

Rosenblatt, L. (1970) *Literature as Exploration*, London: Heinemann

Safran, L. (2001) 'Creativity as "Mindful" Learning', in A. Craft, B. Jeffrey and M. Leibling (eds) *Creativity in Education*, London: Continuum

Said, E. (2003) 'A Window on the World', in *The Guardian* (02/08/03)

Salzberger-Wittenberg, I., Henry, G. and Osborne, E. (1983) *The Emotional Experience of Teaching and Learning*, London: Routledge

Schmidt, M. (ed.) (1980) *Eleven British Poets*, London: Methuen

Sedgwick, F. (2001) *Teaching Literacy: A Creative Approach*, London: Continuum

Segal, S. (1998) 'The Role of Contingency and Tension in the Relationship Between Theory and Practice in the Classroom', *Journal of Curriculum Studies*, 30 (2): 199–206

Shor, I. and Pari, C. (eds) (1999) *Education is Politics: Critical Teaching Across Differences*, Portsmouth NH: Boynton/Cook

Sidgwick, H. (1868) 'The Theory of Classical Education', in *Essays on a Liberal Education*, London: Macmillan

Snyder, I. (1997) 'Hyperfiction: Its Possibilities for English', *English in Education*, 31 (2): 23–33

Spender, S. (1952) 'The Making of a Poem', in B. Ghiselin (ed.) *The Creative Process*, London and New York: Mentor

Stannard, R. (1997) 'Navigating Cyberspace: Vision, Textuality and the World Wide Web', *English in Education*, 31 (2): 14–22

Stead, C. K. (1964) *The New Poetic: Yeats to Eliot*, London: Hutchinson

Stevens, D. (2000) 'William Blake in Education: A Poet for Our Times?', *Changing English*, 7 (1): 55–63

Tate, C. (ed.) (1985) *Black Women Writers at Work*, Harpenden: Old Castle Books

Tate, N. (1995) 'What is Education For?', *English in Education*, 33 (2): 5–18

Traherne, T. (*c.*1660; ed Margolioth 1960) *Centuries*, London: Mowbray

Tripp, D. (1993) *Critical Incidents in Teaching: The Development of Professional Judgement*, London: Routledge

Turkle, S. (1995) *Life on the Screen – Identity in the Age of the Internet*, New York: Simon and Shuster

Tweddle, S. (1995) 'A Curriculum for the Future – A Curriculum Built for Change', *English in Education*, 31 (2): 5–13

Tweddle, S., Adams, A., Clarke, S., Scrimshaw, P. and Walton, S. (1997) *English for Tomorrow*, Buckingham: Open University Press

Voiskounsky, A. (2001) 'Internet Culture in Russia', in W. Frindte, T. Köhler, P. Marquet, E. Nissen (eds) *Internet-based Teaching and Learning (IN-TELE) 99*, Frankfurt am Main: Peter Lang

Vygotsky, L. (1976) 'Play and its Role in the Mental Development of the Child', in J. S. Bruner, A. Jolly and K. Sylva (1976) (eds) *Play: Its Role in Development and Evolution*, Harmondsworth: Penguin

Warnock, M. (1976) *Imagination*, London: Faber and Faber

White, J. (1907) *The Educational Ideas of Froebel*, London: University Tutorial Press

Willans, G. and Searle, R. (1985) *The Compleet Molesworth*, London: Pavilion Books

Willis, P. (1979) *Learning to Labour*, Aldershot: Gator

Wittgenstein, L. (1922; this edn 1994) 'Tractatus Logico-Philosophicus', in A. Kenny (ed.) *The Wittgenstein Reader*, Oxford: Blackwell

Woods, P. (2001) 'Creative Literacy', in A. Craft, B. Jeffrey and M. Leibling (eds) *Creativity in Education*, London: Continuum

Wu, D. (ed.) (1998) *Romanticism: An Anthology*, Oxford: Blackwell

Young, R. (1989) *A Critical Theory of Education: Habermas and Our Children's Future*, New York: Harvester Wheatsheaf

Zancanella, D., Hall, L. and Pence, P. (2000) 'Computer Games as Literature', in A. Goodwyn (ed.) *English in the Digital Age: Information and Communications Technology and the Teaching of English*, London and New York: Cassell

Index

eBooks

eBooks – at www.eBookstore.tandf.co.uk

A library at your fingertips!

eBooks are electronic versions of printed books. You can store them on your PC/laptop or browse them online.

They have advantages for anyone needing rapid access to a wide variety of published, copyright information.

eBooks can help your research by enabling you to bookmark chapters, annotate text and use instant searches to find specific words or phrases. Several eBook files would fit on even a small laptop or PDA.

NEW: Save money by eSubscribing: cheap, online access to any eBook for as long as you need it.

Annual subscription packages

We now offer special low-cost bulk subscriptions to packages of eBooks in certain subject areas. These are available to libraries or to individuals.

For more information please contact webmaster.ebooks@tandf.co.uk

We're continually developing the eBook concept, so keep up to date by visiting the website.

www.eBookstore.tandf.co.uk

DATE DUE

FEB 2 1 2005		
FEB 0 1 REC'D		
JAN 2 8 REC'D		
OhioLINK		
JUN 1 5 REC'D		
MAY 0 4 2010		
APR 1 7 REC'D		

WITHDRAWN

GAYLORD | | | PRINTED IN U.S.A.

LB 1631 .S737 2004

Stevens, David, 1952-

The art of teaching
secondary English